LETTERHEAD & LOGO DESIGNS

CREATING THE CORPORATE IMAGE

LISA WALKER
STEVE BLOUNT

Published by Rockport Publishers
Distributed by North Light Books
1507 Dana Avenue
Cincinnati, Ohio 45207
1-800-289-0963

Designed and Produced by
Blount & Walker Visual Communications, Inc.
8771 Larwin Lane
Orlando, Florida 32817
(407) 677-6303

Authors/Editors
Lisa Walker
Steve Blount

Photography
Nick Lilavois

Associate Designer
H.T. Klaus Heesch

Published by
Rockport Publishers
5 Smith Street
Rockport, MA 01966
(508) 546-9590

Distributed to the trade in the U.S. and Canada by
North Light, an imprint of F&W Publications
1507 Dana Avenue
Cincinnati, OH 45207
(800) 289-0963
(513) 531-2222

Distributed to the trade throughout the rest of the world by
Hearst Books International
105 Madison Avenue
New York, NY 10016
(212) 481-0355

Other distribution by
Rockport Publishers
5 Smith Street
Rockport, MA 01966
(508) 546-9590
Telex: 5106019284
Fax: (508) 546-7141

ISBN 0-935603-37-9

ACKNOWLEDGEMENT

This book could not have been produced without the generous cooperation of the many designers whose work is featured. They not only permitted its reproduction, but dug deep into their personal archives and connected us with their colleagues so that this collection would indeed represent the very best recent work in the field of logotype and stationery design. Our sincere thanks to you all.

CONTENTS
CLIENTS

DESIGN FIRMS

DESIGNERS

DESIGNERS

Client: Pongo Productions
Design Firm: Hitman of Design
Designers: Tracy McGoldrick, Richard Newsome
Art Director: Robert Fusfield
Paper/Printing: Stationery: Two colors on recycled paper;
Business Card: Two colors on mar-coated stock

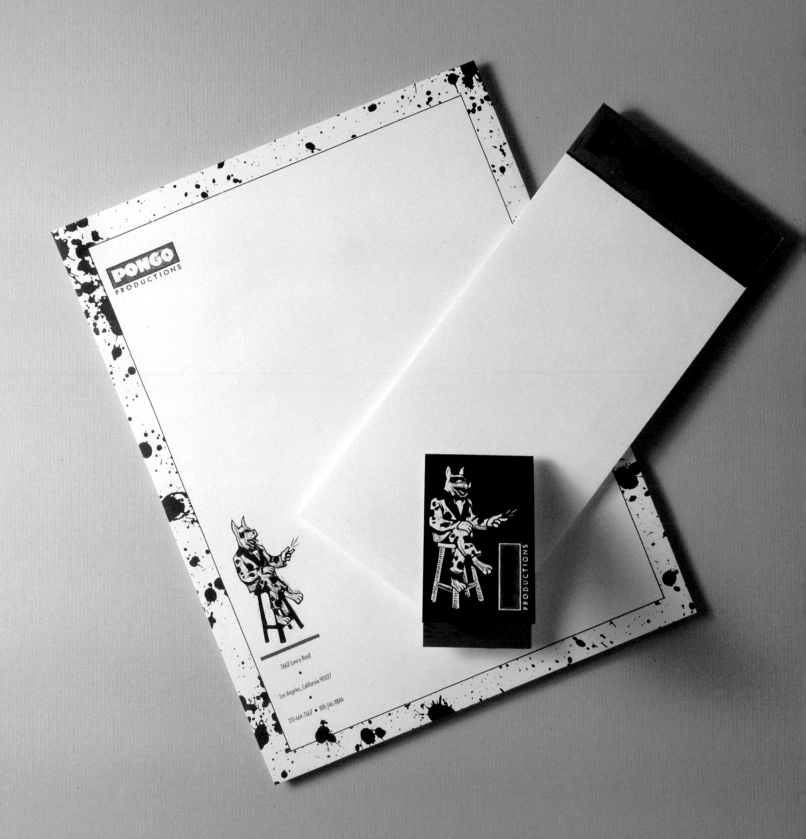

Client: Zonk Inc.
Design Firm: Tracy Sabin, Illustration & Design
Designer: Tracy Sabin
Paper/Printing: Stationery: Two colors on 70-lb. Avon Brilliant White Classic Crest Text; Business Card: Two colors on 80-lb. Avon Brilliant White Classic Crest Cover; Envelope: One color on 60-lb. Astrobrite Neptune Blue

Client: Swim Quik Cruisewear
Design Firm: Muller + Company
Designer: Patrice Eilts
Art Director: Patrice Eilts
Paper/Printing: Stationery: Three colors (2/1) on Foxriver Techniclear 25 percent cotton rag.
Business Cards, greeting cards and bag: Four colors (3/1) on Kromecoat C1S.
The pattern was created in matte peach ink, the logo in gloss ink.

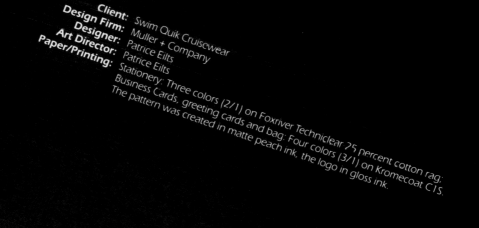

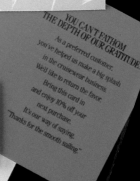

Colour Techniques Limited
17 Avon Trading Estate
Avonmore Road Kensington
London W14 8TS
Telephone 01-602•2936 and 2941

T R A N S P A R E N C Y   R E T O U C H I N G   P H O T O C O M P O S I T E S   A N D   D U P L I C A T E S

Registered in England No. 2002827 Registered office 154 Marsh Road Leagrave Luton LU3 2QL Directors Roy K. Olney Robert J.G. Bloomfield (Managng)

Client: Stockworks
Design Firm: Stan Evenson Design
Designer: Stan Evenson
Art Director: Stan Evenson
Paper/Printing: One color with screened art on Classic Crest

Client: B.D. Fox & Friends, Inc.
Design Firm: B.D. Fox & Friends, Inc.
Designer: Robert Biro
Art Directors: Brian D. Fox, Robert Biro
Paper/Printing: Four colors on 24 lb. Quintessence Bright White

B.D. FOX & FRIENDS, INC.
ADVERTISING
1111 BROADWAY
SANTA MONICA, CA 90401
213-394-7150
FAX 213-393-1569

B.D. FOX & FRIENDS, INC.
ADVERTISING
1111 BROADWAY
SANTA MONICA, CA 90401
213-394-7150

B.D. FOX & FRIENDS, INC.
ADVERTISING
1111 BROADWAY
SANTA MONICA, CA 90401
213-394-7150

B.D. FOX & FRIENDS, INC.
ADVERTISING
1111 BROADWAY
SANTA MONICA, CA 90401
213-394-7150

Client: Cymbal Crown Inc.
Design Firm: The Bradford Lawton Design Group
Designer: Bradford Lawton
Art Directors: Bradford Lawton, Ellen Pullen
Paper/Printing: Three colors on Protocol Brite White Woven, 25 percent cotton

Client: Tracy Sabin
Design Firm: Tracy Sabin, Illustration & Design
Designer: Tracy Sabin
Paper/Printing: All pieces printed on French Speckletone. Stationery: Three colors on Chalk White Text; Business Card: Two colors on Grenoble Gray Cover; Envelopes: One color on Briquet Text

TRACY SABIN, ILLUSTRATION & DESIGN / 13476 RIDLEY RD., SAN DIEGO, CA 92129 / (619) 484-8712

Client: Orlando Cabanban Photography
Design Firm: Goldsmith Yamasaki Specht Inc.
Designer: Daniel Karp
Art Director: Claude Cummings
Paper/Printing: Two colors on Curtis Brightwater Smooth

Clients: Roger Christian, Bill West
Design Firm: Taylor/Christian Advertising
Designer: Roger Christian
Art Director: Roger Christian
Paper/Printing: Six colors on 24-lb. Protocol Writing White Wove

Cabanban

Orlando Cabanban Photography

539 South Plymouth Court Suite 105
Chicago, Illinois 60605
Phone 312.922.1830

?..............!

IDEAS THAT WORK.

TAYLOR/CHRISTIAN ADVERTISING, INC.
16115 BRIDGEWOOD
SAN ANTONIO, TEXAS 78248
(512) 829-4360
FAX 829-4973

MANHATTAN COOKING / SERENA BASS

DESIGNED TO PRINT
+ ASSOCIATES, LTD.

145 West 13th Street New York, N.Y. 10011 212 741-9646

DESIGN AND MARKETING CONSULTANTS
130 WEST 25th STREET • NEW YORK, NY 10001 • (212) 924-2090

Client: Manhattan Cooking Company
Design Firm: Julie Losch Design
Designer: Julie Losch
Paper/Printing: Two colors on 24-lb. Strathmore Writing
Bright White Wove

Client: Designed To Print + Associates
Design Firm: Designed To Print + Associates
Designer: Tree Trapanese
Art Directors: Tree Trapanese, Peggy Leonard, David Un
Paper/Printing: Two colors on Strathmore Esprit Brite White

Client: Kiddo
Design Firm: Barnes Design Office
Designer: Jeff A. Barnes
Art Director: Jeff A. Barnes
Paper/Printing: One color on Strathmore Writing Bright White Wove

2639 NORTH HALSTED
CHICAGO, ILLINOIS 60614
312-975-6977
A DIVISION OF HOT DUDS, INC.

Client: Big Drum
Design Firm: Elmwood Design Limited
Designer: Gary Swindell
Art Director: Gary Swindell
Paper/Printing: Stationery: Two colors on Tullis Russell Mellotex Smooth Ultra White;
Business Cards: Two colors on Taffeta Ivory Board White

WITH COMPLIMENTS

big drum.

BIG DRUM, DAVIS HOUSE, 29 HATTON GARDEN, LONDON EC1N 8DA. TELEPHONE 01-430 0362. FAX 01-831 0799.
ALSO AT: ELMWOOD HOUSE, GHYLL ROYD, GUISELEY, LEEDS LS20 9LT.

big drum.

MIKE RENWICK
ILLUSTRATION DIRECTOR

ELMWOOD HOUSE
GHYLL ROYD
GUISELEY, LEEDS LS20 9LT
TELEPHONE 0943 870229
FAX 0943 870191

big drum.

BIG DRUM, DAVIS HOUSE, 29 HATTON GARDEN, LONDON EC1N 8DA. TELEPHONE 01-430 0362. FAX 01-831 0799.
ALSO AT: ELMWOOD HOUSE, GHYLL ROYD, GUISELEY, LEEDS LS20 9LT.
ELMWOOD DESIGN LTD. REG NO 1274703 ENGLAND.

Client: Verbi
Design Firm: Veistola Oy Advertising Agency
Designer: Jukka Veistola
Art Director: Jukka Veistola

Client: Texaco USA
Design Firm: Anspach Grossman Portugal
Designer: Kenneth Love
Art Director: Kenneth Love
Paper/Printing: Two colors on special white stock with Texaco watermark

J H Lindblom   **Texaco USA**   PO Box 52332
Manager   Houston TX 77052
Marketing Engineering   713 650 5082

Texaco USA   P O Box 52332
                    Houston TX 77052-2332

FORM S-112 7-84

Texaco USA   P O Box 52332
                    Houston TX 77052

J H Lindblom   **Texaco USA**
Manager   Marketing
Marketing Engineering   1111 Rusk Street
                          PO Box 52332
                          Houston TX 77052
                          713 650 5082

22

Client: Rob Wellington Quigley
Design Firm: CWA, Inc./Humangraphic
Designer: Calvin Woo
Art Director: Calvin Woo
Paper/Printing: Two colors on Cranes Crest

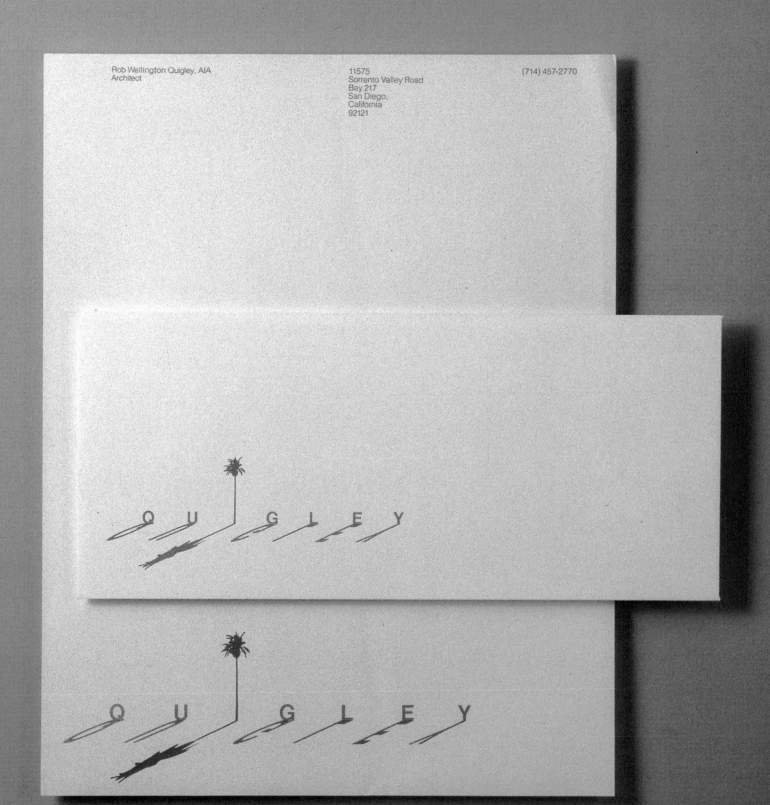

Rob Wellington Quigley, AIA
Architect

11575
Sorrento Valley Road
Bay 217
San Diego,
California
92121

(714) 457-2770

Client: Dallas Repetory Theatre
Design Firm: Peterson & Company
Designer: Scott Ray
Art Director: Scott Ray
Paper/Printing: Two colors on Protocol Warm Gray

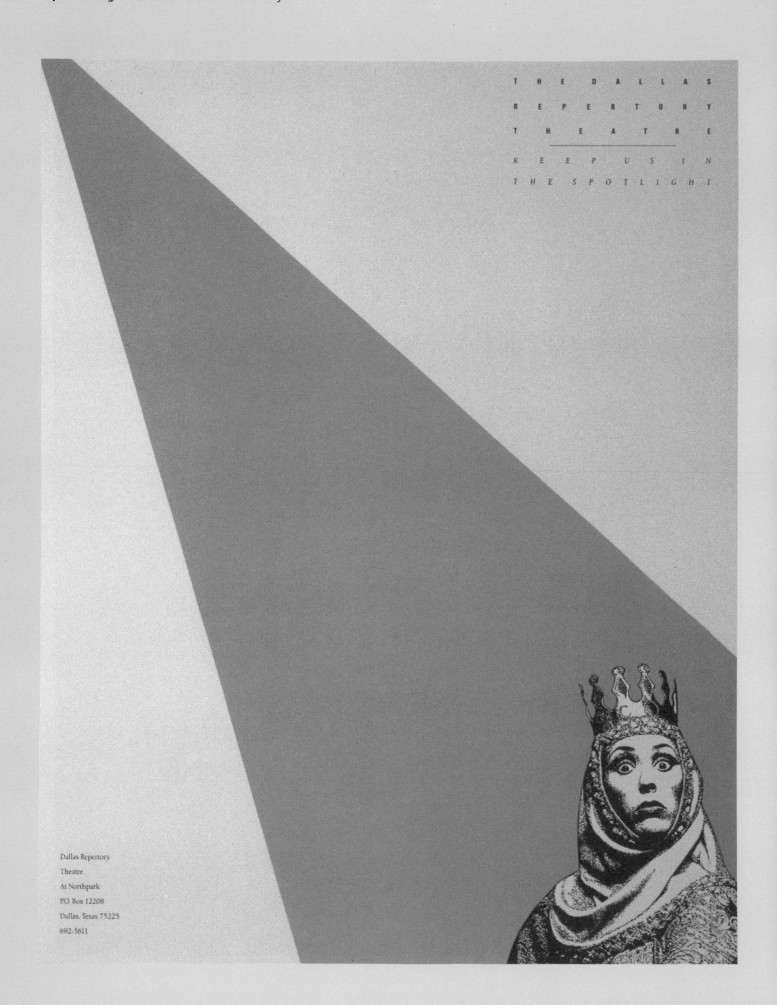

THE DALLAS
REPERTORY
THEATRE
KEEP US IN
THE SPOTLIGHT

Dallas Repertory
Theatre
At Northpark
P.O. Box 12208
Dallas, Texas 75225
692-5611

Client: Bruce Hands Photography
Design Firm: Hornall Anderson Design Works
Designers: Jack Anderson, Cliff Chung, Rey Sabad
Art Director: Jack Anderson

**BRUCE HANDS
PHOTOGRAPHER**
P.O. BOX 16186
SEATTLE, WA 98116-0186
(206) 938-8620

Client: Parelle Sportive/Parcours, Inc.
Design Firm: Shiffman Young Design Group
Designer: Meryl Pollen
Art Director: Tracey Shiffman
Paper/Printing: Two colors on Crane Dalton Bond

Client: Sunrise Preschool
Design Firm: Richardson or Richardson
Designers: Forrest Richardson, Valerie Richardson
Art Directors: Forrest Richardson, Valerie Richardson
Paper/Printing: Two colors on 28-lb. Strathmore Writing White Wove

Client: Intershirt AG
Design Firm: Geissbühler AGI
Designer: Geissbühler AGI

Client: G.E. Frye Co.
Design Firm: James Bright & Company
Designer: Hugh Dunnahoe
Art Director: James Bright
Paper/Printing: Three colors on Classic Crest Dorian Grey

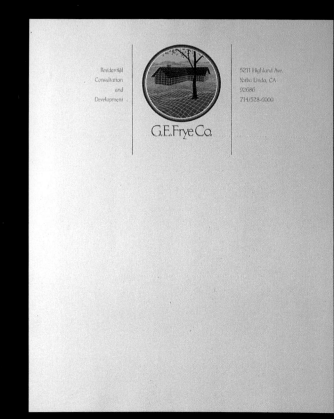

Client: Janet Bevan International
Design Firm: John Nash & Friends
Designer: Mark Pearce
Art Director: John Nash
Paper/Printing: Two colors

Client: Interior Design Service
Design Firm: Image Design, Inc.
Designer: Howard Diehl
Art Director: Howard Diehl
Paper/Printing: One color plus foil stamping on Classic Crest Dorian Grey

Client: Telluride Film Festival/The National Film Preserve, Ltd.
Design Firm: Georganna Towne Graphic Design
Designer: Georganna Towne
Art Director: Georganna Towne
Paper/Printing: Three colors on 70-lb. Champion Pagaentry Smooth White Text

A presentation of The National Film Preserve, Ltd.; a tax-exempt nonprofit educational corporation

14 South Main Street   Box B1156   Hanover, NH 03755   USA
Telephone (603)643-1255   Fax (603)643-5938

Client: Rowdy Creative, Inc.
Design Firm: Rowdy Creative, Inc.
Designers: Chuk Batko, Paul Hagen
Art Directors: Chuk Batko, Paul Hagen
Paper/Printing: Three colors, embossed on Protocol Writing White

Client: Frederick R. Weisman Art Foundation
Design Firm: Shiffman Young Design Group
Designer: Tracey Shiffman
Art Director: Tracey Shiffman
Paper/Printing: Four colors on Strathmore Writing White

Client: Hybrinetics, Inc.
Design Firm: Image Group, Inc.
Designer: Dave Bacigalupi
Art Director: Tom Armstrong

Client: The Uhlman Company
Design Firm: Muller & Company
Designer: Patrice Eilts
Art Directors: Patrice Eilts, Scott Chapman

Client: Fischee Real Estate
Design Firm: Gormley & Welker Graphic Design
Designer: Tim Gormley
Art Director: Steve Welker

Client: Skagit Citizens for Nuclear Disarmament
Design Firm: Galen Design Associates
Designers: Larry Galen Larson, Pat Davis
Art Director: Larry Galen Larson

Client: Skagit Valley Tulip Festival
Design Firm: Galen Design Associates
Designer: Larry Galen Larson
Art Director: Larry Galen Larson

Client: Romantically Yours
Design Firm: Lanny Sommese Design
Designer: Kristin Breslin
Art Director: Carl Mill

SPICES

Client: Spices Restaurant
Design Firm: Carter Wong Limited
Designer: Phillip Wong
Art Director: Phillip Wong

Client: Unity School
Design Firm: UCI, Inc.
Designer: Roy Urano
Art Director: Roy Urano

ROMANTICALLY
yours

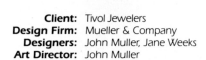

The Tivol annual Picnic & Volleyball Blowout

Client: Ak▪Sar▪Ben Racetrack
Design Firm: Mueller & Company
Designer: Patrice Eilts
Art Director: Patrice Eilts

Client: Tivol Jewelers
Design Firm: Mueller & Company
Designers: John Muller, Jane Weeks
Art Director: John Muller

Client: Penn State Glee Club
Design Firm: Lanny Sommese Design
Designers: Lanny Sommese, Kristin Breslin
Art Director: Lanny Sommese

Client: Dutch Opera/Falstaff
Design Firm: Samenwerkende
Designer: André Toet
Art Director: André Toet

Client: Willis Painting
Design Firm: Richards Brock Miller Mitchell
Designer: D.C. Stipp
Art Director: D.C. Stipp

Client: Witte Museum/Camel Corps
Design Firm: The Bradford Lawton Group
Designers: Bradford Lawton
Art Director: Bradford Lawton

Client: Kim Bunch Productions
Design Firm: The Bradford Lawton Group
Designers: Bradford Lawton
Art Director: Bradford Lawton

TEXAS CAMEL CORPS

WITTE EXPEDITIONS TO THE FRONTIER & BEYOND

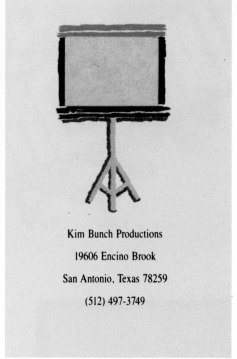

Kim Bunch Productions

19606 Encino Brook

San Antonio, Texas 78259

(512) 497-3749

Client: Hitter & Associates/Malibu Pier
Design Firm: David Westwood & Associates
Designer: David Westwood
Art Director: David Westwood

1

2

3

4

1	**Client:**	Wavedancer	5	**Client:**	Ueda/Seta Associates	9	**Client:**	Bob Coonts Design Group
	Design Firm:	Tharrington Graphics		**Design Firm:**	UCI, Inc.		**Design Firm:**	Bob Coonts Design Group
	Designer:	Alan Tharrington		**Designer:**	Ryo Urano, Dan Sato		**Designer:**	Greg Rattenborg
	Art Director:	Alan Tharrington		**Art Director:**	Ryo Urano		**Art Director:**	Bob Coonts

2	**Client:**	Headline International	6	**Client:**	Gritz Visual Graphics	10	**Client:**	Patrick SooHoo Designers
	Design Firm:	They Design		**Design Firm:**	Bob Coonts Design Group		**Design Firm:**	Patrick SooHoo Designers
	Designer:	Mark Smith, Guido Brouwers		**Designer:**	Doug Post		**Designer:**	Patrick SooHoo
	Art Director:	Mark Smith, Guido Brouwers		**Art Director:**	Doug Post		**Art Director:**	Patrick SooHoo

3	**Client:**	Tharrington Graphics	7	**Client:**	Tidwell Landscape Architecture	11	**Client:**	Margaret Watson
	Design Firm:	Tharrington Graphics		**Design Firm:**	Shiffman Young Design Group		**Design Firm:**	Peterson & Company
	Designer:	Alan Tharrington		**Designer:**	Tracey Shiffman		**Designer:**	Bryan Peterson
	Art Director:	Alan Tharrington		**Art Director:**	Tracey Shiffman		**Art Director:**	Bryan Peterson

4	**Client:**	Stroud	8	**Client:**	Exact	12	**Client:**	Eric Behrens
	Design Firm:	They Design		**Design Firm:**	Jukka Veistola		**Design Firm:**	Wendy Behrens Design
	Designer:	Guido Brouwers		**Designer:**	Jukka Veistola		**Designer:**	Wendy Behrens
	Art Director:	Guido Brouwers		**Art Director:**	Jukka Veistola		**Art Director:**	Wendy Behrens

5

Ueda/Seta Associates, INC.
Commercial & Residential Interiors

Ritsuko Seta A.S.I.D.

851 Pohukaina Street, Building C, Bay 3
Honolulu, Hawaii 96813
Ph: (808) 524-3950 Fax: (808) 528-3415

6

James Gritz

GRITZ

GRITZ VISUAL GRAPHICS
5595 Arapahoe Road
Boulder, CO 80303
(303) 449-3840

Fine Lithography and
Screen Printing

7

landscape architecture

8

EXACT

BIRGITTA WULFF

EXACT – MANTILA & WULFF OY AB.
ENGELINAUKIO 13 A. 00150 HELSINKI. PUH. 622 1716 & 622 1706. TELEFAX. 622 1702

9

TI BENSEN
Creative Director

BOB COONTS DESIGN GROUP

234 WALNUT ST. P.O. BOX 6335
FT. COLLINS, COLORADO 80525
303 · 493 · 3181 FORT COLLINS
303 · 444 · 8490 DENVER METRO.

10

8800
Venice
Boulevard
Suite A
Los
Angeles
CA
90034
213
856
8800
Fax
839
3039

11

MARGARET

WATSON

REPRESENTS

6631 SAN MATEO

DALLAS, TX 75223

214 328 9216

12

E·B

ERIC BEHRENS
PHOTOGRAPHER
1 NEWS PLAZA
PEORIA, IL
309.686.3137

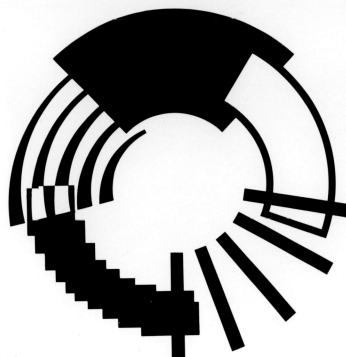

Client: Hogeschool voor de Kunsten Utrecht
Design Firm: Samenwerkende Ontwerpers
Designer: Jan Paul de Vries
Art Director: André Toet

Client: K2 Skis
Design Firm: Hornall Anderson Design Works
Designers: Jack Anderson, Jani Drewfs, David Bates
Art Director: Jack Anderson

Client: Dante's Restaurant, Inc.
Design Firm: Lanny Sommese Design
Designer: Kristin Breslin
Art Director: Lanny Sommese

Client: Asymetrix Corporation
Design Firm: Hornall Anderson Design Works
Designers: Jack Anderson, Juliet Shen, Heidi Hatlestad
Art Director: Jack Anderson

Client: All British Field Meet
Design Firm: Hornall Anderson Design Works
Designers: Jack Anderson, David Bates
Art Director: Jack Anderson

Client: Studio 904 Mayor's Award
Design Firm: Hornall Anderson Design Works
Designers: Juliet Shen, Heidi Hatlestad
Art Director: Juliet Shen

Client: GTE-SMU Athletic Forum
Design Firm: Peterson & Company
Designer: Scott Ray
Art Director: Scott Ray
Paper/Printing: Two colors

. . .

Doak
Walker
Award

The Doak
Walker
Award/
GTE-SMU
Athletic
Forum
3000 Daniel
Dallas, TX
75205
214-987-3712

. . .

The National
Running
Back Award

. . .

Doak Walker
Award
National
Selection
Board:
Tony Barnhart
Earl Campbell
John David Crow
Dick Enberg
Keith Jackson
Tom Landry
Malcolm Moran
Jim Nantz
Walter Payton
Gale Sayers
Brad Sham
Ed Sherman
Blackie Sherrod
Roger Staubach
Doak Walker
Gene Wojciechowski

. . .

Doak
Walker
Award

Client: Palmier Bistro
Design Firm: CWA, Inc./Humangraphic
Designer: Susan Merritt
Art Director: Calvin Woo
Paper/Printing: Two colors plus emboss on Strathmore Bright White Wove

Client: Nelson Entertainment
Design Firm: B.D. Fox & Friends, Inc.
Designer: Garrett Burke
Art Directors: Brian D. Fox, Garrett Burke
Paper/Printing: One color on white bond

NELSON
ENTERTAINMENT
335 North Maple Drive · Suite 350
Beverly Hills, California 90210

PETER D. GRAVES
Senior Vice President

335 North Maple Drive
Beverly Hills
CA 90210-3899
213-285-6150
Fax 213-285-6190

NELSON
ENTERTAINMENT

335 North Maple Drive · Suite 350 · Beverly Hills, California 90210 · 213-285-6000 · Fax 2132856190 · Telex 4938846

Client: The American Tobacco Company
Design Firm: Peterson & Blyth Associates
Designer: David Scarlett
Art Director: David Scarlett
Paper/Printing: One color on white bond

Client: Tim Girvin Design, Inc.
Design Firm: Tim Girvin Design, Inc.
Designer: Robin Rickabaugh
Art Director: Tim Girvin
Paper/Printing: One color on Cranes Crest White Wove with hand-rendered accents;
Business Cards: 80-lb. Karma Cover Natural

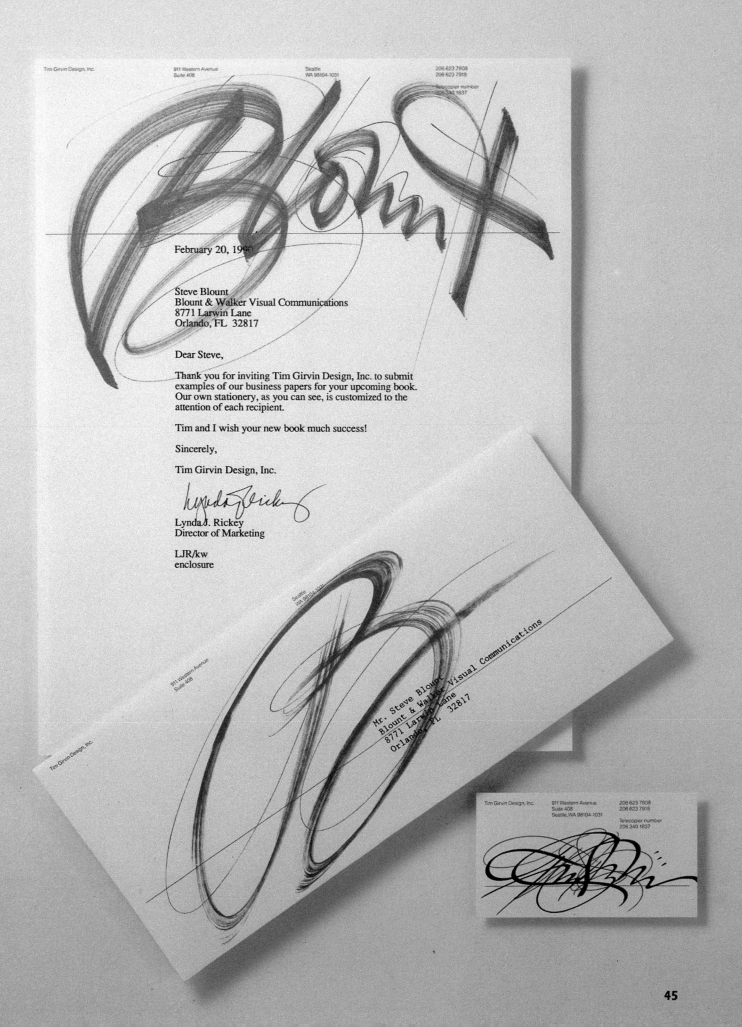

Client: Deborah Zemke Illustration
Design Firm: Deborah Zemke Illustration
Designer: Deborah Zemke
Art Director: Deborah Zemke
Paper/Printing: Two colors on Protocol Warm White

Client: Information Research
Design Firm: Hitman of Design
Designers: Robert Fusfield, Gail Johnson, Richard Newsome
Paper/Printing: Stationery & Envelope: Strathmore Bright White;
Business Cards & Folder: 100-lb. Quintessence cover with a dull varnish;
Mailing Labels: Matte label stock

Client: Intempo Toys
Design Firm: Russell Leong Design
Designers: Russell K. Leong, Pam M. Matsuda
Art Director: Russell K. Leong
Paper/Printing: Black and three PMS colors on 24-lb. Protocol Bright White, wove finish

P.O. Box 50157
Palo Alto, California
94303

415.324.2502

Dan and Bev Mjolsness
Rural Route Two
Red Wing, MN 55066
612. 388. 3811

THOROUGHBRED BREEDING AND RACING

Client: Tarmac EZD
Design Firm: Leslie Millard Associates
Designer: Les Causton
Art Director: Les Causton
Paper/Printing: Three colors on white bond stock

— THE —
N≋WS
CRUMBLES

— THE —
CRUMBL≋S
HARBOUR · VILLAGE

CRUMBLES HARBOUR VILLAGE LIMITED
COMPTON ESTATE OFFICE
COMPTON PLACE ROAD, EASTBOURNE
EAST SUSSEX BN21 1EB
TELEPHONE: 0323 648825 FACSIMILE: 0323 648893

Client: Gormley & Welker
Design Firm: Gormley & Welker Graphic Design
Designer: Tim Gormley
Art Director: Steve Welker
Paper/Printing: Stationery: Two colors on 24-lb. Strathmore Writing;
Business Card: Two colors on 80-lb. Cover

Client: Apple Design Source, Inc.
Design Firm: Apple Design Source, Inc.
Designer: Marta Houser
Art Director: Barry Seelig
Paper/Printing: Two colors on 24-lb. Neenah Classic Linen Avon Brilliant White

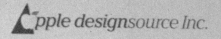

Client: Gloria Ferrer
Design Firm: Colonna, Farrell: Strategic Marketing & Design
Designer: John Farrell
Paper/Printing: One color, gold foil stamping and blind embossing on white Strathmore Writing

Donna Brown
Accountant · Office Manager

P.O. BOX 1427 · 23555 HWY. 121
SONOMA, CALIFORNIA 95476
(707) 996-7256

P.O. BOX 1427 · 23555 HWY. 121 · SONOMA, CALIFORNIA 95476 (707) 996-7256

Client: The Canine Company
Design Firm: Richardson or Richardson
Designer: Forrest Richardson
Art Directors: Forrest Richardson, Valerie Richardson
Paper/Printing: One color on Simpson Kilmory 1776

Client: Dr. T's Music Software
Design Firm: Ruby Shoes Studio
Designer: Susan Tyrrell
Art Director: Susan Tyrrell
Paper/Printing: Two colors with a screen on Curtis Flannel Wedgewood Blue

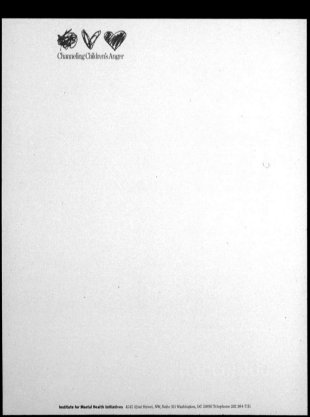

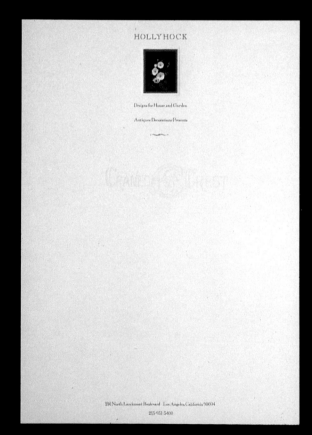

Client: Institute for Mental Health Initiatives
Design Firm: Shapiro Design Associates Inc.
Designer: Terri Bogaards
Art Director: Ellen Shapiro
Paper/Printing: Two colors on Simpson Protocol

Client: Hollyhock
Design Firm: Michael Brock Design
Designers: Michael Brock, Gaylen Braun
Art Director: Michael Brock
Paper/Printing: One color and debossed panel on 32-lb. Cranes Crest Wove Finish

Client: Murray Johnstone
Design Firm: McIlroy Coates Ltd.
Designer: Andrew Hunter
Paper/Printing: Two colors on 100 gsm blade-coated Cartridge

MURRAY
JOHNSTONE

Murray Managed Exempt Fund
Managers: Murray Johnstone Unit Trust Management Limited
7 West Nile Street, Glasgow G1 2PX, Telephone 041-226 3131, Telex 778667
Fax 041-248 5420

Member of IMRO and LAUTRO
Registered Office: 7 West Nile Street, Glasgow G1 2PX, Registered in Scotland Number 65167

Client: Elmwood Design Limited
Design Firm: Elmwood Design Limited
Designer: Ray Conlon
Art Director: Ray Conlon
Paper/Printing: Stationery: Two colors on GB Brightwater Arctic;
Business Cards: Two colors on Chalfont Ivory Board White

ELMWOOD

ELMWOOD

JONATHAN P. SANDS

MANAGING DIRECTOR

ELMWOOD DESIGN LIMITED, ELMWOOD HOUSE, GHYLL ROYD, GUISELEY,
LEEDS LS20 9LT. TEL: 0943 870229 (8 LINES). FAX: 0943 870191.
ALSO AT: DAVIS HOUSE, 29 HATTON GARDEN, LONDON EC1N 8DA.
TEL: 01 430 0362. FAX: 01 831 0799. | PART OF THE CHARLES WALLS GROUP.

ELMWOOD

WITH|COMPLIMENTS

ELMWOOD DESIGN LIMITED, ELMWOOD HOUSE, GHYLL ROYD, GUISELEY, LEEDS LS20 9LT. TEL: 0943 870229 (8 LINES). FAX: 0943 870191.
ALSO AT: DAVIS HOUSE, 29 HATTON GARDEN, LONDON EC1N 8DA. | PART OF THE CHARLES WALLS GROUP.

ELMWOOD DESIGN LIMITED, ELMWOOD HOUSE, GHYLL ROYD, GUISELEY, LEEDS LS20 9LT. TEL: 0943 870229 (8 LINES). FAX: 0943 870191.
REG NO: 1274703 ENGLAND.

Client: Sharpe Illusions
Design Firm: Image Group, Inc.
Designer: Deborah Cunninghame-Blank
Art Director: Deborah Cunninghame-Blank
Paper/Printing: Stationery and Envelope: Four colors on 24-lb. Classic Crest Avon Brilliant White text;
Business Cards: Four colors on high-gloss Kromekote White Cover

Client: Rowland Ranches/Louis Rowland
Design Firm: The Bradford Lawton Design Group
Designers: David Hackney, Jody Laney
Art Director: Bradford Lawton
Paper/Printing: Six colors on Speckletone Writing

Client: Spontaneous Combustion
Design Firm: Muller + Company
Designer: Patrice Eilts
Art Director: Patrice Eilts
Paper/Printing: One color on French Speckletone -Kraft

Client: Minnesota Society of the American Institute of Architects
Design Firm: Rubin Cordaro Design
Designer: William Homan
Art Director: Bruce Rubin
Paper/Printing: 24-lb. Protocol Writing Bright White Wove

Client: Facère
Design Firm: Hornall Anderson Design Works
Designers: Jack Anderson, Cliff Chung
Art Director: Jack Anderson

Client: G&G Realty Partners, Inc.
Design Firm: Bullet Communications
Designer: Tim Scott
Art Director: Tim Scott
Paper/Printing: Two colors on 24-lb. Curtis Brightwater
Writing Bright White

Client: Brass Tacks Interiors
Design Firm: Carter Wong Limited
Designer: Alison Tomlin
Art Director: Alison Tomlin
Paper/Printing: Four-color process on Connoisseur

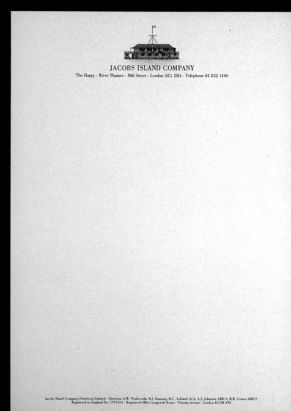

Client: Julian Bicycle Company & Touring
Design Firm: Henson Design Associates
Designer: Chip Henson
Art Director: Chip Henson
Paper/Printing: Two colors with a 10 percent screen on
Classic Crest Natural White

Client: Jacobs Island Company
Design Firm: John Nash & Friends
Designer: John Nash
Art Director: John Nash
Paper/Printing: Four-color process

Client: Donna Daguanno + Associates
Design Firm: Barnes Design Office
Designer: Jeff A. Barnes
Art Director: Jeff A. Barnes
Paper/Printing: Two colors on Crane Crest

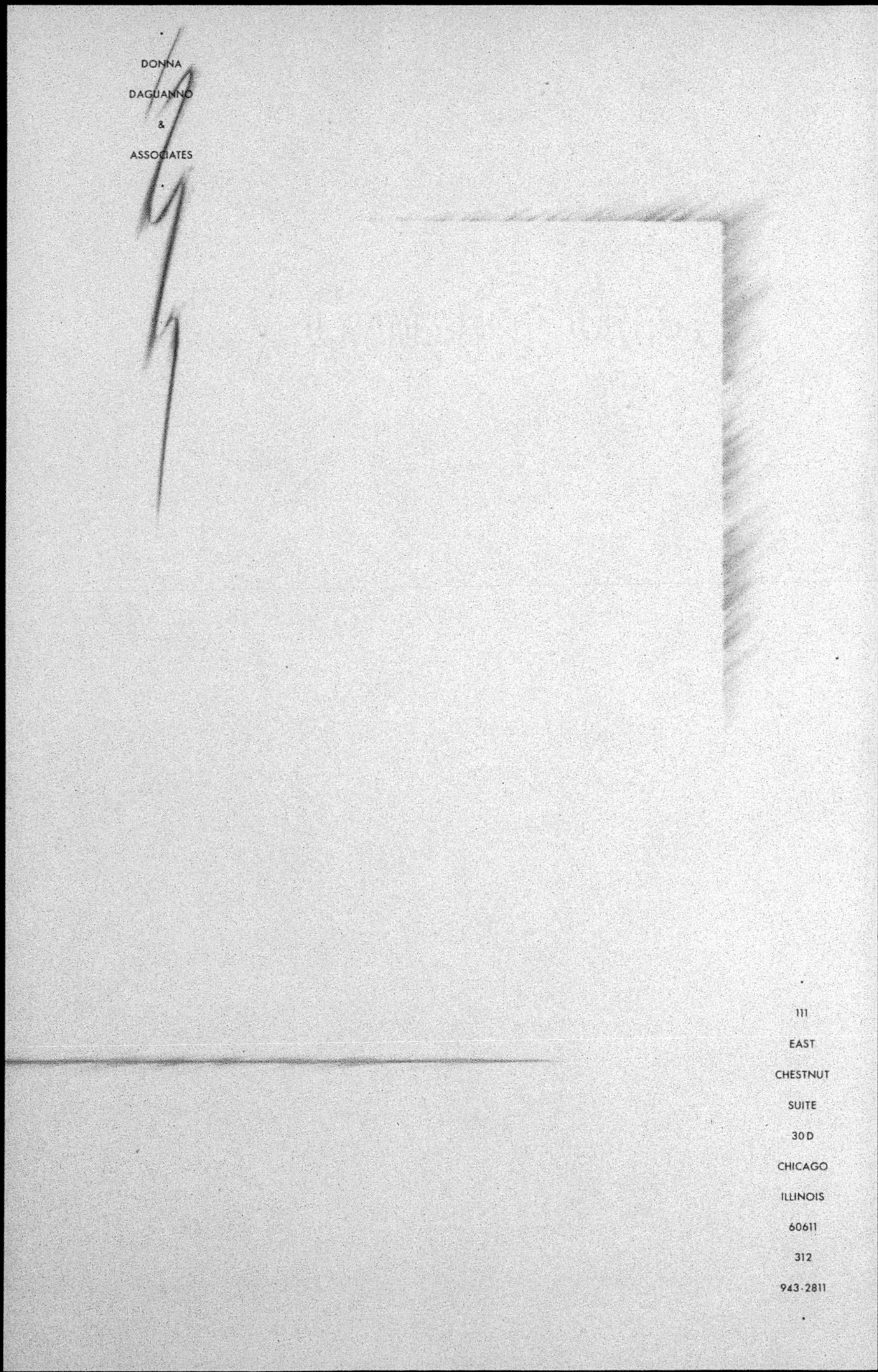

DONNA

DAGUANNO

&

ASSOCIATES

111

EAST

CHESTNUT

SUITE

30 D

CHICAGO

ILLINOIS

60611

312

943-2811

Client: China Link
Design Firm: Primo Angeli, Inc.
Designer: Philippe Becker
Art Director: Primo Angeli
Paper/Printing: One color on white Cranes Crest

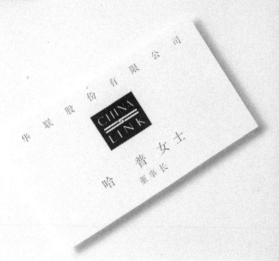

Client: Scripto Tokai
Design Firm: Peterson & Blyth Associates
Designer: Peterson & Blyth Associates
Art Director: Ronald Peterson
Paper/Printing: Two colors on Classic Laid White

Client: Groupe Ma
Design Firm: Catherine Zask
Designer: Catherine Zask
Paper/Printing: Three colors

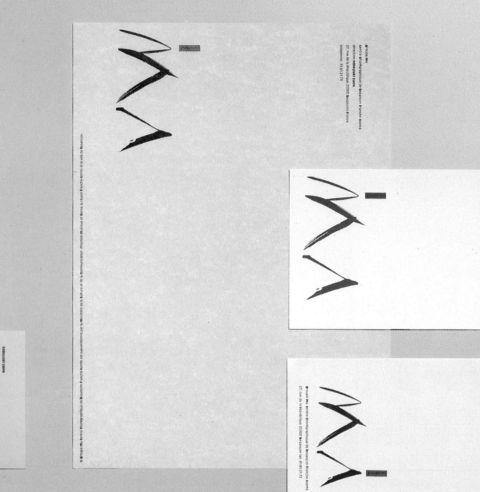

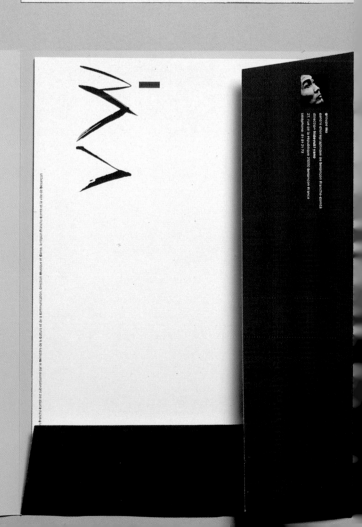

Client: Shigeru Akizuki
Design Firm: Shigeru Akizuki
Designer: Shigeru Akizuki
Paper/Printing: Envelopes: Lightweight paulownia wood, can be mailed at standard postal rate

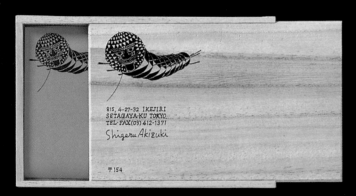

Letterhead Designs 1
Blount & Company
No. 12 Station Rd.
Cranbury, NJ 08512

Client: TDCTJHTBIPC
Design Firm: The Weller Institute for the Cure of Design
Designer: Don Weller
Art Director: Don Weller
Paper/Printing: Strathmore Writing

Client: Chiasso
Design Firm: Barnes Design Office
Designer: Jeff A. Barnes
Art Director: Jeff A. Barnes
Paper/Printing: Two colors on Strathmore Writing Bright White Wove

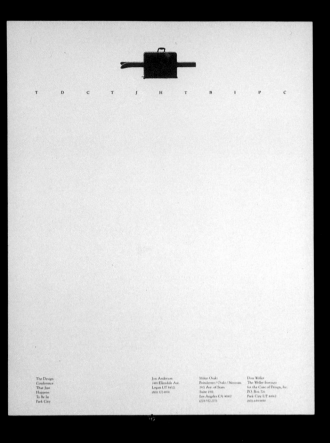

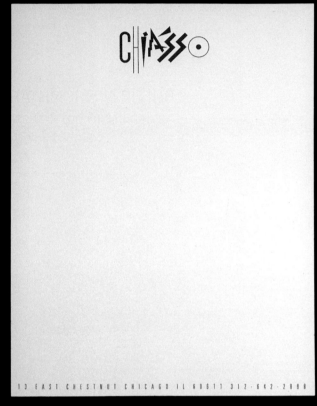

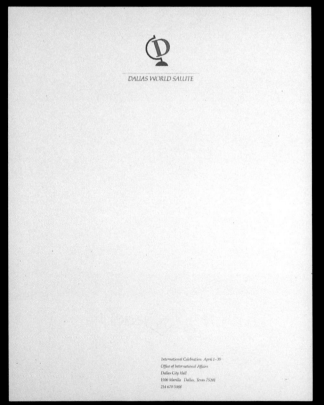

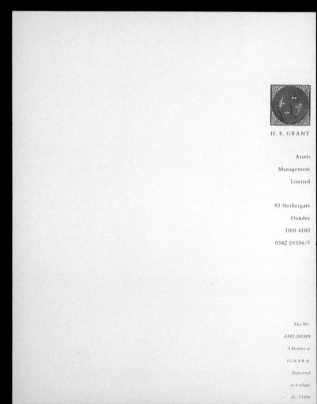

Client: Office of International Affairs, Dallas City Hall
Design Firm: RBMM/Richards Group
Designer: Gary Templin
Art Director: Gary Templin
Paper/Printing: Two colors on Cranes Crest Sub. 241 Wove

Client: H.E. Grant Assets Management Ltd.
Design Firm: McIlroy Coates
Designers: Aird McKinstrie, David James
Art Director: Linda Farquharson
Paper/Printing: Four colors on White Classic Wove

Client: Cafe Lulu
Design Firm: Muller + Company
Designer: Patrice Eilts
Art Directors: Patrice Eilts, John Muller
Paper/Printing: All pieces except invitation: Two colors on 100-lb. White Warren Cover Lustro Dull;
Invitation: Two colors on 80-lb. White Starwhite Vicksburg

Client: Dahlquist Illustration
Design Firm: Dahlquist Illustration
Designer: Roland Dahlquist
Art Director: Roland Dahlquist
Paper/Printing: Stationery: Two colors on 28-lb. Classic Crest Avon Brilliant White;
Business Card: Two colors on 80-lb. Cover Avon Brilliant White

Client: Cohen Freedman Associates
Design Firm: Cahan & Associates
Designer: Patricia McShane
Art Director: Bill Cahan
Paper/Printing: Two colors and tint varnish on 24-lb. Strathmore Writing Bright White Wove

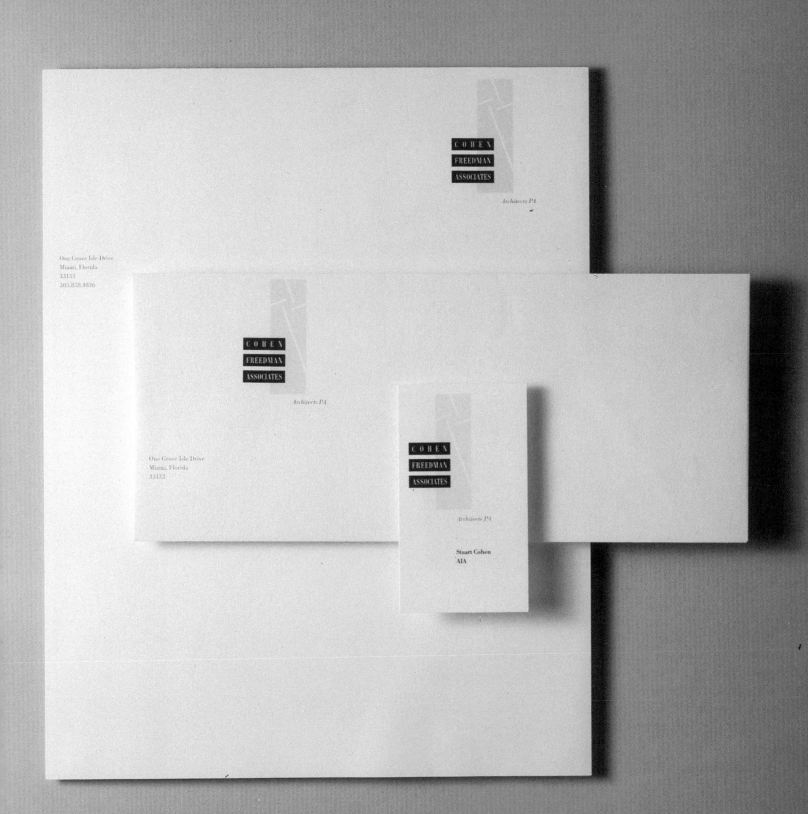

Client: T.V. Australia
Design Firm: Raymond Bennett Design Pty. Ltd.
Designer: Raymond Bennett
Art Director: Raymond Bennett
Paper/Printing: Two colors on 100 gsm Conqueror White Laid

Client: TV 25/Educable
Design Firm: Rickabaugh Graphics
Designer: Tina Zientarski
Art Director: Eric Rickabaugh
Paper/Printing: Two colors on Strathmore Bright White Wove

Client: Ruby Shoes Studio, Inc.
Design Firm: Ruby Shoes Studio, Inc.
Designers: Karen Watkins, Susan Tyrrell
Art Director: Susan Tyrrell
Paper/Printing: Two colors on Strathmore Bright White Wove

Client: Port Miolla Associates, Inc.
Design Firm: Port Miolla Associates, Inc.
Designer: Port Miolla Associates
Art Directors: Paul Port, Ralph Miolla
Paper/Printing: Two colors on Strathmore Bright White Wove

Johnson

Productions

8035
Broadway
San Antonio
Texas
78209

5 1 2   8 2 9   4200
San Antonio

2 1 4   8 6 9   4414
Dallas

5 1 2   8 2 9   4266
Fax

Johnson   Michael Taylor
Producer

Productions

P r o d u c t i o n s   4200
San Antonio
5 1 2   8 2 9   4414
Dallas
2 1 4   8 6 9   4266
Fax
5 1 2   8 2 9

JOHSON

Johnson

Productions

8035
Broadway
San Antonio
Texas
78209

JOH SON

JOHNSON

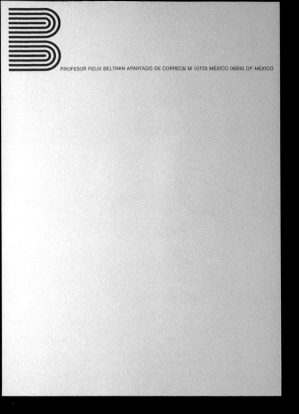

PROFESOR FELIX BELTRAN APARTADO DE CORREOS M 10733 MEXICO 06000 DF MEXICO

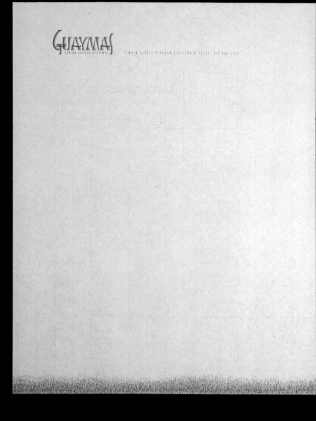

GUAYMAS

THE KLINKAM COMPANY

Construction
Management

735 Skinner Building
Fifth Avenue
Seattle, WA
98101
(206) 624-9795

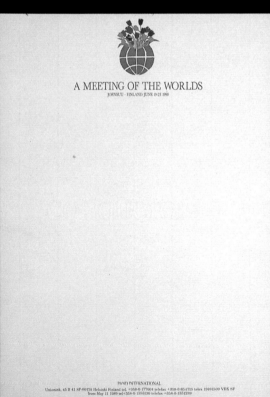

A MEETING OF THE WORLDS
JOENSUU · FINLAND JUNE 19-25 1990

PAND INTERNATIONAL
Unioninkatu 45 B 41 SF-00170 Helsinki Finland tel. +358-0-177001 telefax +358-0-654715 telex 191015000 VDX SF
from May 11 1989 tel +358-0-1355130 telefax +358-0-1351239

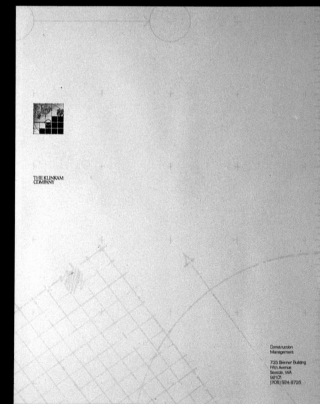

Client: Pand International
Design Firm: Veistola Oy Advertising Agency
Designer: Jukka Veistola
Art Director: Jukka Veistola

Client: The Klinkam Company
Design Firm: Hornall Anderson Design Works
Designers: Jack Anderson, Jani Drewfs
Art Director: Jack Anderson

C O N T O U R

L I G H T I N G

Contour Lighting Limited 32 Raynham Road, Bishop's Stortford, Hertfordshire CM23 5PE Telephone: 0279 506647

Registered in England No. 172 835I Registered Office: Waterloo Chambers, Waterloo Lane, Chelmsford, Essex CM1 1BD

Client: Numa...
Design Firm: Kenichi Sam...
Designer: Kenichi Samura
Art Director: Kenichi Samura

Client: Hall Grey Architects
Design Firm: Royle-Murgatroyd Design Ltd.
Designers: Royle-Murgatroyd Design Ltd.
Art Director: Keith Murgatroyd

Client: Typhoon Pictures Ltd.
Design Firm: Graphic Communication Ltd.
Designer: Henry Steiner
Art Director: Henry Steiner
Paper/Printing: Conqueror white laid

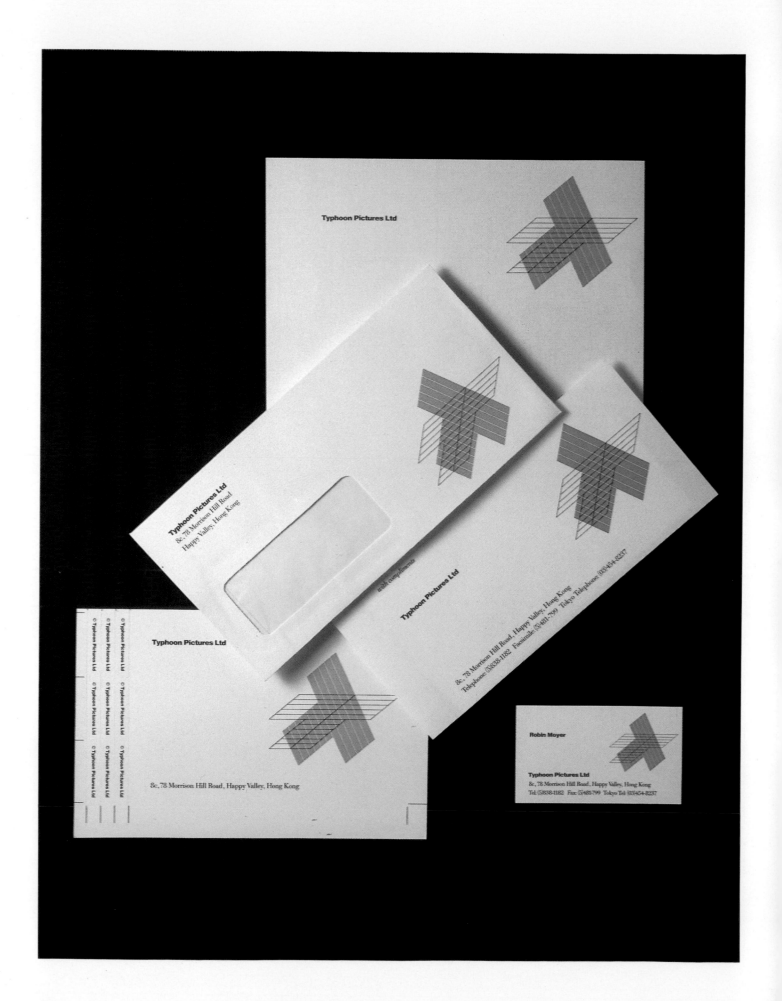

Client: Russell Leong Design
Design Firm: Russell Leong Design
Designer: Russell K. Leong
Art Director: Russell K. Leong
Paper/Printing: Stationery and envelope: Four colors on 24-lb. Protocol Bright White
Business Card: Four colors on 88-lb. Protocol Plus Cover

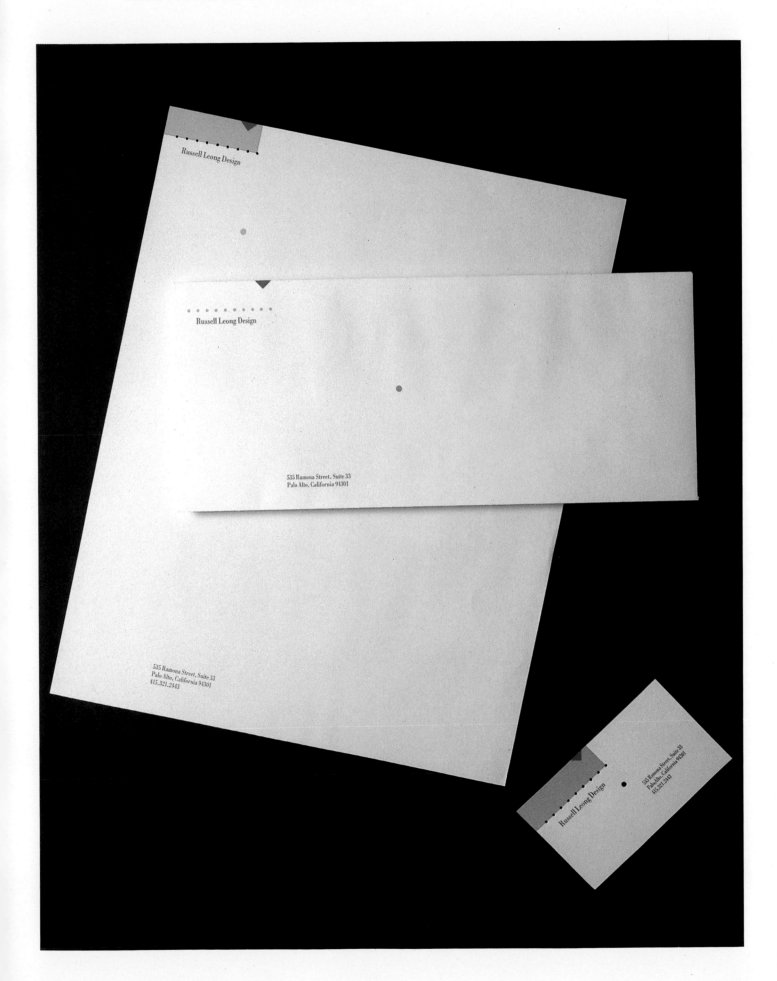

Client: Mirage
Design Firm: Hornall Anderson Design Works
Designers: Jack Anderson, Mark McGowan
Art Director: Jack Anderson

Client: Minneapolis Chapter of the American Institute of Architects
Design Firm: Rubin Cordaro Design
Designer: William Homan
Art Director: Bruce Rubin
Paper/Printing: 24-lb. Protocol Writing Bright White Wove

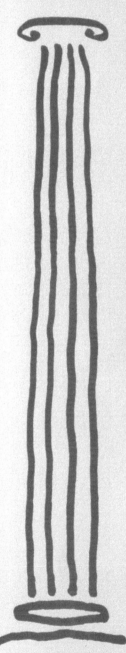

MINNEAPOLIS
CHAPTER
•
AMERICAN
INSTITUTE OF
ARCHITECTS

275 MARKET
STREET
SUITE 54
MINNEAPOLIS
MN 55405
612/338-6763

Client: Raymond Bennett
Design Firm: Raymond Bennett Design Pty. Ltd.
Designer: Raymond Bennett
Art Director: Raymond Bennett
Paper/Printing: Stationery: Two colors on Kilmory stock,
Business Cards: Two colors on 31- gsm white art board

Raymond
Bennett
Design.

Invoice

Raymond
Bennett
Design

Date   Job No.

Client

Description

Please return artwork to:
Raymond Bennett Design Pty Ltd First Floor Nine Myrtle Street Crows Nest NSW Australia 2065
Telephone (02) 959 5777 Facsimile (02) 922 5790

Raymond
Bennett
Design

Date   Order No   Invoice No

Raymond
Bennett
Design

Raymond Bennett Design Pty Ltd
9 Myrtle Street Crows Nest NSW Australia 2065
Telephone (02) 959 5777 Facsimile (02) 922 5790

Raymond
Bennett
Design

With Compliments

Raymond
Bennett
Design

Raymond Bennett
Managing Director

Raymond Bennett Design Pty Ltd
First Floor Nine Myrtle Street
Crows Nest NSW Australia 2065
Telephone (02) 959 5777 Facsimile (02) 922 5790

Raymond Bennett Design Pty Ltd First Floor Nine Myrtle Street Crows Nest NSW Australia 2065 Telephone (02) 959 5777 Facsimile (02) 922 5790

Terms: Nett 7 days.   E. & O.E.
Raymond Bennett Design Pty Ltd First Floor Nine Myrtle Street Crows Nest NSW Australia 2065 Telephone (02) 959 5777 Facsimile (02) 922 5790

Client: Los Angeles Sports Council
Design Firm: Bright & Associates
Designers: Ray Wood (logo), Wilson Ong (stationery)
Art Director: Keith Bright
Paper/Printing: Printed in six colors

Los Angeles
Sports Council

404 South Bixel Street
Los Angeles, CA 90017
USA
213-629-0613
FAX 213-629-0708

NEWS

Los Angeles
Sports Council

404 South Bixel Street
Los Angeles, CA 90017
USA
213-629-0613
FAX 213-629-0708

Los Angeles
Sports Council

404 South Bixel Street
Los Angeles, CA 90017
USA

Client: Signature Cycles
Design Firm: Gormley & Welker Graphic Design
Designer: Steve Welker
Art Director: Tim Gormley
Paper/Printing: Stationery: Two colors on 24-lb. Strathmore Writing;
Business Card: Two colors on Strathmore 80-lb. Cover

SIGNATURE
cycles

SIGNATURE
cycles

AL WELKER

P.O. BOX 325, SOMERS, N.Y. 10589 (914)248-8941

P.O. BOX 325, SOMERS, N.Y. 10589 (914)248-8941

Client: Shimokochi/Reeves Design
Design Firm: Shimokochi/Reeves Design
Designers: Mamoru Shimokochi, Anne Reeves
Art Directors: Mamoru Shimokochi, Anne Reeves

SHIMOKOCHI

REEVES

DESIGN

Design for

Marketing

4465

Wilshire

Boulevard

Los Angeles

California

90010-3704

Phone:

▶ 213 937 3414

Fax:

213 937 3417

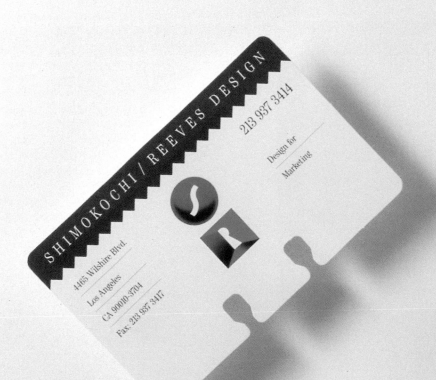

Client: Lines Direct, Inc.
Design Firm: Hugh Dunnahoe Illustration & Design
Designer: Hugh Dunnahoe
Art Director: Hugh Dunnahoe
Paper/Printing: Two colors on Classic Crest Bright White

Client: Wendy Wells
Design Firm: Wells Design
Designer: Wendy Wells
Art Director: Wendy Wells
Paper/Printing: Two colors on Neenah Classic Crest Laid
Bright White Writing

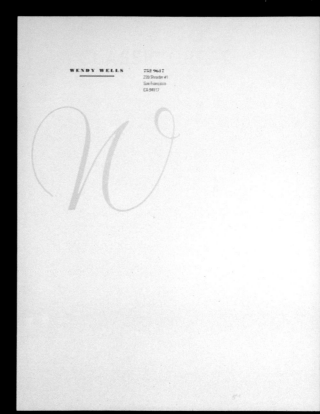

Client: Share Foundation
Design Firm: David Hackney Graphic Design
Designer: David Hackney
Art Director: David Hackney
Paper/Printing: Two colors

Client: Jim Benedict
Design Firm: Taylor/Christian Advertising
Designer: Roger Christian
Art Director: Elaine Lytle
Paper/Printing: Two colors on 24-lb. Protocol Writing White Wove

Client: Grand Cafe Berlage
Design Firm: Vorm Vijf Grafisch Ontwerpteam BNO
Designer: Eric van Casteren
Art Director: Eric van Casteren

Client: Unisys Corporation
Design Firm: Anspach Grossman Portugal
Designer: Robin Andrews
Art Director: Kenneth Love
Paper/Printing: Two colors Nekoosa White Bond

Client: California Avocado Commission
Design Firm: Peterson & Blyth Associates
Designer: Peterson & Blyth Associates
Art Director: Ronald Peterson
Paper/Printing: Two colors plus emboss on Kimberley Writing White Laid

C A L I F O R N I A   A V O C A D O   C O M M I S S I O N

C A L I F O R N I A   A V O C A D O   C O M M I S S I O N

JOHN W. BARTELME
President

C A L I F O R N I A   A V O C A D O   C O M M I S S I O N

C A L I F O R N I A   A V O C A D O   C O M M I S S I O N

17620 Fitch   Irvine, California 92714   714 558-6761   Telex 257817

Client: Hornall Anderson Design Works
Design Firm: Hornall Anderson Design Works
Designers: John Hornall, Jack Anderson, Brian O'Neill
Art Director: Jack Anderson

Client: Jamnastics
Design Firm: Gerhardt & Clemons, Inc.
Designer: Kristie J. Clemons
Art Director: Kristie J. Clemons
Paper/Printing: Stationery: Two colors on 24-lb. Strathmore Writing Bright White Wove

Client: World Debating Championship/Guinness plc
Design Firm: McIlroy Coates
Designer: Iain Lauder
Art Director: Andrew Hunter
Paper/Printing: Two colors on 100 gsm Conqueror Wove

GLASGOW
1 9 9 0

WORLD
DEBATING
CHAMPIONSHIPS

PRINCIPAL SPONSOR
GUINNESS

GLASGOW 1990

GLASGOW
UNIVERSITY UNION
32 UNIVERSITY AVENUE
GLASGOW G12 8LX

TELEPHONE
041 · 334 · 2302

FACSIMILE
041 · 334 · 2216

Design Firm: Vorm Vijf Grafisch Ontwerpteam
Designer: Eric van Casteren
Art Director: Eric van Casteren
Paper/Printing: Two-color process

SPORTSCHOOL

HOUDING- EN FIGUURVERBETERING

CONDITIETRAINING

AEROBIC DANCING

KICK-BOXING

JIU-JITSU

BOKSEN

KARATE

YOGA

JUDO

kees tempel

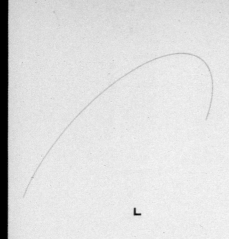

L

I

Willem van Konijnenburglaan 3

5613 DW Eindhoven

Telefoon: (040) 44 70 76

Rabo Eindhoven-Zuid:

11.37.23.601

Postbank: 5487644

Client: Lindell's
Design Firm: Cahan & Associates
Designer: Erik Adigard
Art Director: Bill Cahan
Paper/Printing: Stationery: One color and foil stamping on 24-lb. Neenah Classic Crest Writing
Natural White; Business Card: One color and foil stamping on 80-lb. Neenah
Classic Crest Cover Natural White

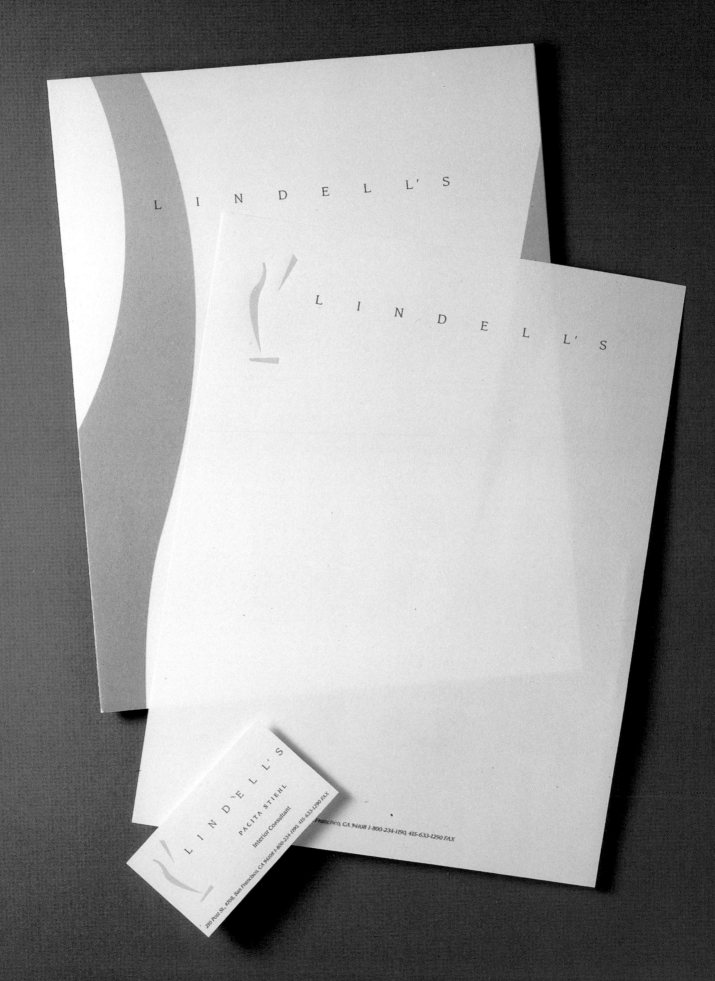

Client: Tumbleweed Restaurant
Design Firm: Michael Brock Design
Designers: Michael Brock, Gaylen Braun
Art Director: Michael Brock
Paper/Printing: Four colors on 24-lb. Speckletone

Client: CBS Inc., FM Broadcast Group
Design Firm: Calico
Designer: Tom Burton
Art Director: Mary Burton

Client: CBS Inc., FM Broadcast Group
Design Firm: Calico
Designer: Ken Leonard
Art Director: Ken Leonard

Client: Warner Cable Communications
Design Firm: Calico, Ltd.
Designer: John Folmer
Art Directors: John Folmer, Joel Fajnor

Client: CBS Inc., FM Broadcast Group
Design Firm: Calico, Ltd.
Designer: Ken Leonard
Art Director: Ken Leonard

Client: Dos Equis
Design Firm: Jamie Davison Design Inc.
Designer: Jamie Davison
Art Director: Jamie Davison

Client: Cloud Mountain Farm
Design Firm: Galen Design Associates
Designer: Larry Galen Larson
Art Director: Larry Galen Larson

VIDEO SEVEN

Client: Video Seven
Design Firm: Jamie Davison Design Inc.
Designer: Jamie Davison
Art Director: Jamie Davison

Client: Jansport
Design Firm: Hornall Anderson Design Works
Designers: Jack Anderson, Jani Drewfs, Cliff Chung
Art Director: Jack Anderson

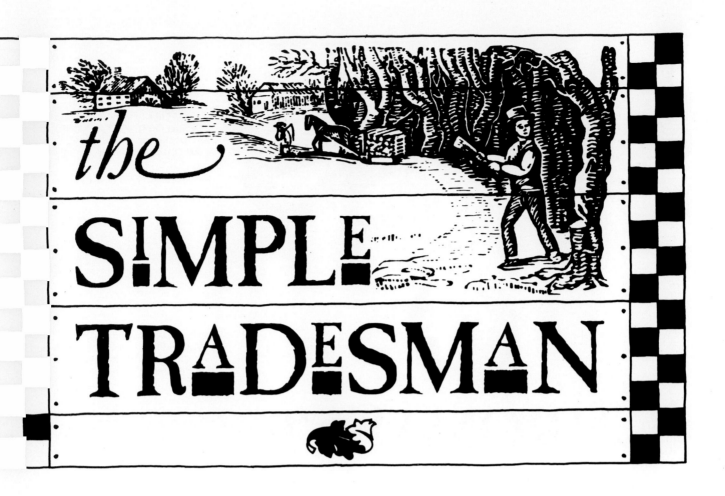

Client: Simple Tradesman
Design Firm: Gormley & Welker Graphic Design
Designer: Tim Gormley
Art Director: Steve Welker

Client: E.B. Walsh Ventures, Inc.
Design Firm: Gormley & Welker Graphic Design
Designer: Tim Gormley
Art Director: Steve Welker

SWING SHIFT PAINTERS

LONGMIRE SPRINGS
GENERAL STORE

Client: Longmire Springs General Store
Design Firm: Hornall Anderson Design Works
Designer: Jack Anderson
Art Director: Jack Anderson

C
CHROMASET

Client: ChromaSet
Design Firm: Jamie Davison Design Inc.
Designer: Jamie Davison
Art Director: Jamie Davison

MOOD INDIGO

Client: Copperfield Company Ltd.
Design Firm: Alan Chan Design Co.
Designers: Alan Chan, Phillip Leong
Art Director: Alan Chan

Client: Future Games
Design Firm: Jamie Davison Design Inc.
Designer: Jamie Davison
Art Director: Jamie Davison

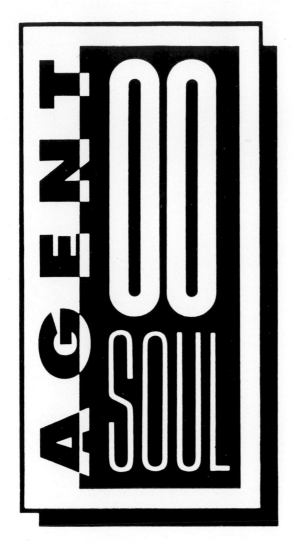

Client: Twist Records
Design Firm: Hitman Of Design
Designers: Kala Kollanyi, Richard Newsome
Art Director: Robert Fusfield

Client: Hong Kong Tourist Association
Design Firm: Graphic Communication Ltd.
Designer: Henry Steiner
Art Director: Henry Steiner

Client: Vintage Bank
Design Firm: Colonna, Farrell: Strategic Marketing & Design
Designer: Ralph Colonna

Client: Milwaukee Institute of Art & Design
Design Firm: Frankenberry, Laughlin & Constable, Inc.
Designer: Mark Koerner
Art Director: Mark Koerner
Paper/Printing: Three colors on Classic Linen

Client: Mithun Partners
Design Firm: Hornall Anderson Design Works
Designers: Jack Anderson, Cliff Chung, Brian O'Neill
Art Director: Jack Anderson

M

MITHUN
PARTNERS

M

MITHUN
PARTNERS

STEPHEN W. COX, AIA
ASSOCIATE

ARCHITECTURE
PLANNING &
INTERIOR DESIGN
2000 112TH AVE NE
BELLEVUE WA 98004
(206) 454 3344
FAX (206) 646 4776

ARCHITECTURE
PLANNING &
INTERIOR DESIGN
2000 112TH AVE NE
BELLEVUE WA 98004
(206) 454 3344
FAX (206) 646 4776

M

MITHUN
PARTNERS

ARCHITECTURE
PLANNING &
INTERIOR DESIGN

Client: Leonidas
Design Firm: Vorm Vijf Grafisch Ontwerpteam
Designer: Paul Scholte
Art Director: Paul Scholte

Client: Edinburgh District Council
Design Firm: McIlroy Coates
Designer: Craig Hutton
Art Director: Andrew Hunter
Paper/Printing: Three colors plus tints on 100 gsm Conqueror Wove

Client: Spectacles/John E. Hendry
Design Firm: McIlroy Coates
Designer: Lizzie Sanders
Art Director: Lizzie Sanders
Paper/Printing: Two colors on Connoisseur Hammer Finish

Client: Los Films del Camino
Design Firm: Koniszczer Sapoznik Diseñadores Graficos
Designers: Marcelo Sapoznik, Gustavo Koniszczer

Oscar Kramer

Libertad 1213 - 2º
1012 Buenos Aires
Argentina
Teléfonos 41-0885/6801
Télex 25858 CINEIN AR

LOS
FILMS
DEL
CAMINO

Libertad 1213 - 2º
1012 Buenos Aires
Argentina
Teléfonos 41-0885/6801
Télex 25858 CINEIN AR

Client: Thunder Road Adolescent drug treatment centers/Randy Snowden
Design Firm: Ortega Design
Designer: Joann Ortega
Art Director: Joann Ortega
Paper/Printing: Two colors and hot-foil stamping on Filare Naturale White

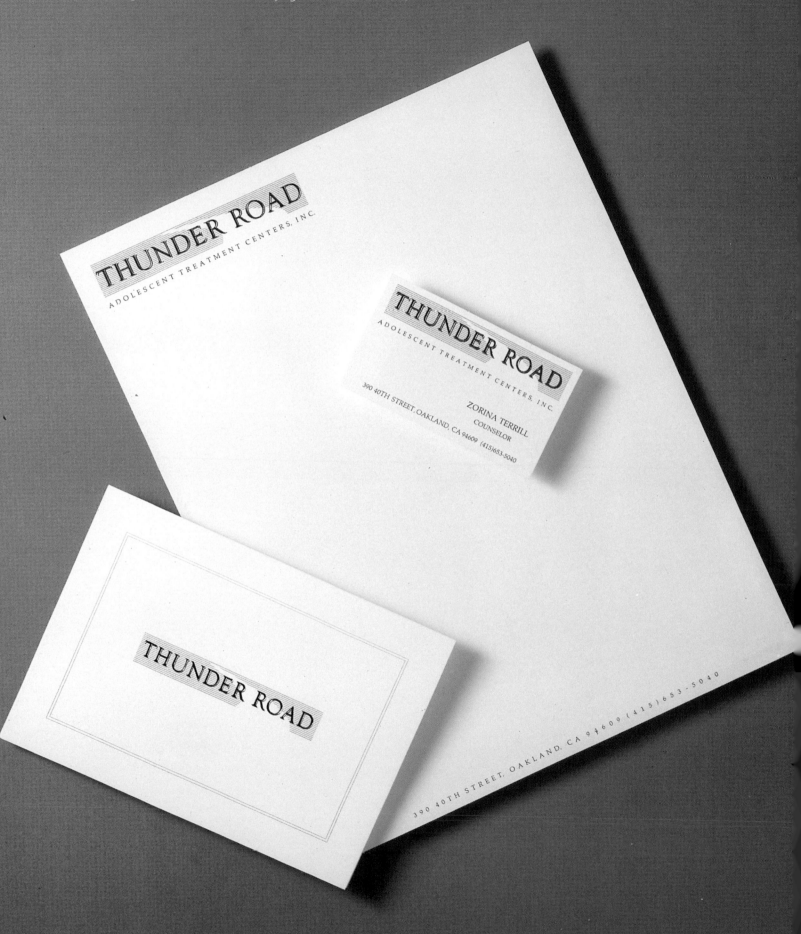

Client: Natural Association of Student Personnel Administrators
Design Firm: Fusion Design Associates
Designer: Fred Knapp
Art Director: Fred Knapp
Paper/Printing: Three colors on 20-lb. Speckletone Chalk White

Client: Clelland Associates, Architects
Design Firm: Wings Design Consultants
Designer: Sav Evangelou
Art Director: Malcolm Park
Paper/Printing: Four colors plus gloss varnish on 135 gsm Highland Matte

CLELLAND ASSOCIATES

ARCHITECTS

CLELLAND ASSOCIATES

ARCHITECTS

WITH COMPLIMENTS

SECOND FLOOR
WASHINGTON HOUSE
50 WASHINGTON STREET
GLASGOW G3 8AZ
TELEPHONE 041 204 3993
FAX 041 204 3988

SECOND FLOOR
WASHINGTON HOUSE
50 WASHINGTON STREET
GLASGOW G3 8AZ
TELEPHONE 041 204 3993
FAX 041 204 3988

Client: John Rizzo Photography
Design Firm: Conge Design
Designer: Bob Conge
Art Director: Bob Conge
Paper/Printing: Three colors on 24-lb. Curtis Flannel Writing White, Felt Finish;
Business Card: Curtis Flannel cover

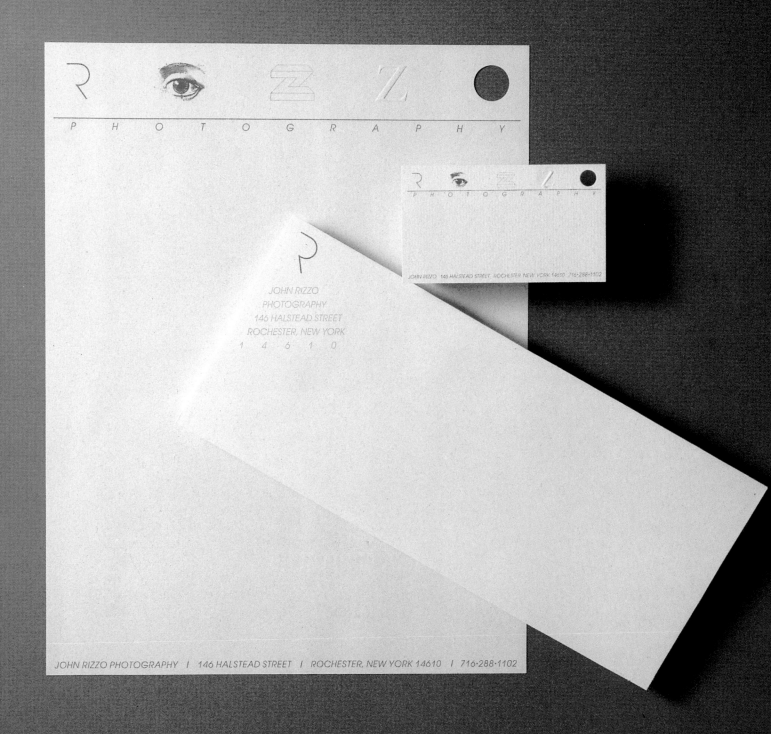

Client: Mass-Observation
Design Firm: John Nash & Friends
Designer: John Nash
Art Director: John Nash
Paper/Printing: Two colors

Client: Lincoln Park Dental Associates
Design Firm: Bullet Communications
Designer: Tim Scott
Art Director: Tim Scott
Paper/Printing: Two colors engraved on 24-lb. Protocol
Writing Soft Blue Wove

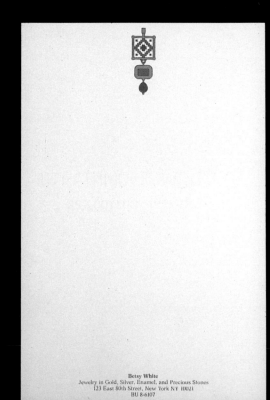

Client: Mannerheimin Lastensuojeluliitto
Design Firm: Veistola Oy Advertising Agency
Designer: Jukka Veistola
Art Director: Jukka Veistola

Client: Betsy White
Design Firm: Shapiro Design Associates Inc.
Designers: Ellen Shapiro, Mark Huie
Art Director: Ellen Shapiro
Paper/Printing: Three colors on Strathmore Writing Natural

Design Firm: Geissbuhler AGI
Designer: K.D. Geissbuhler
Art Director: K.D. Geissbuhler
Paper/Printing: Two colors

RADIO ZÜRICHBERG HÖHENWEG 12 CH-8032 ZÜRICH

TELEFON 01/55 31 72

AUF 101,3 MEGA-HERZ

Client: Ostrobonita Restaurant
Design Firm: Jukka Veistola
Designer: Jukka Veistola
Art Director: Jukka Veistola
Paper/Printing: Three colors

Client: Graphic Communication Ltd.
Design Firm: Graphic Communication Ltd.
Designer: Henry Steiner
Art Director: Henry Steiner
Paper/Printing: One color plus two color foils on gray Conqueror Laid

Client: David Martinez Photography
Design Firm: Tolleson Design
Designer: Steven Tolleson
Art Director: Steven Tolleson
Paper/Printing: Two colors

Client: Tom King Associates Ltd.
Design Firm: Graphic Communication Ltd.
Designer: Henry Steiner
Art Director: Henry Steiner
Paper/Printing: Silver foil stamping on Conqueror Gray Laid

Client: Jean Hillson
Design Firm: Ruby Shoes Studio
Designer: Lisa Smith
Art Director: Susan Tyrrell
Paper/Printing: Two colors with a screen on Strathmore Bright White

APPLIED IMAGINATION

Training to foster ingenious thinking and problem-solving

P.O. Box 800, Cambridge, MA 02140, 617-35-IDEAS

Client: The Graphic Team
Design Firm: Veistola Oy Advertising Agency
Designers: Jukka Veistola, Sakiri Kinnuneri
Art Director: Jukka Veistola

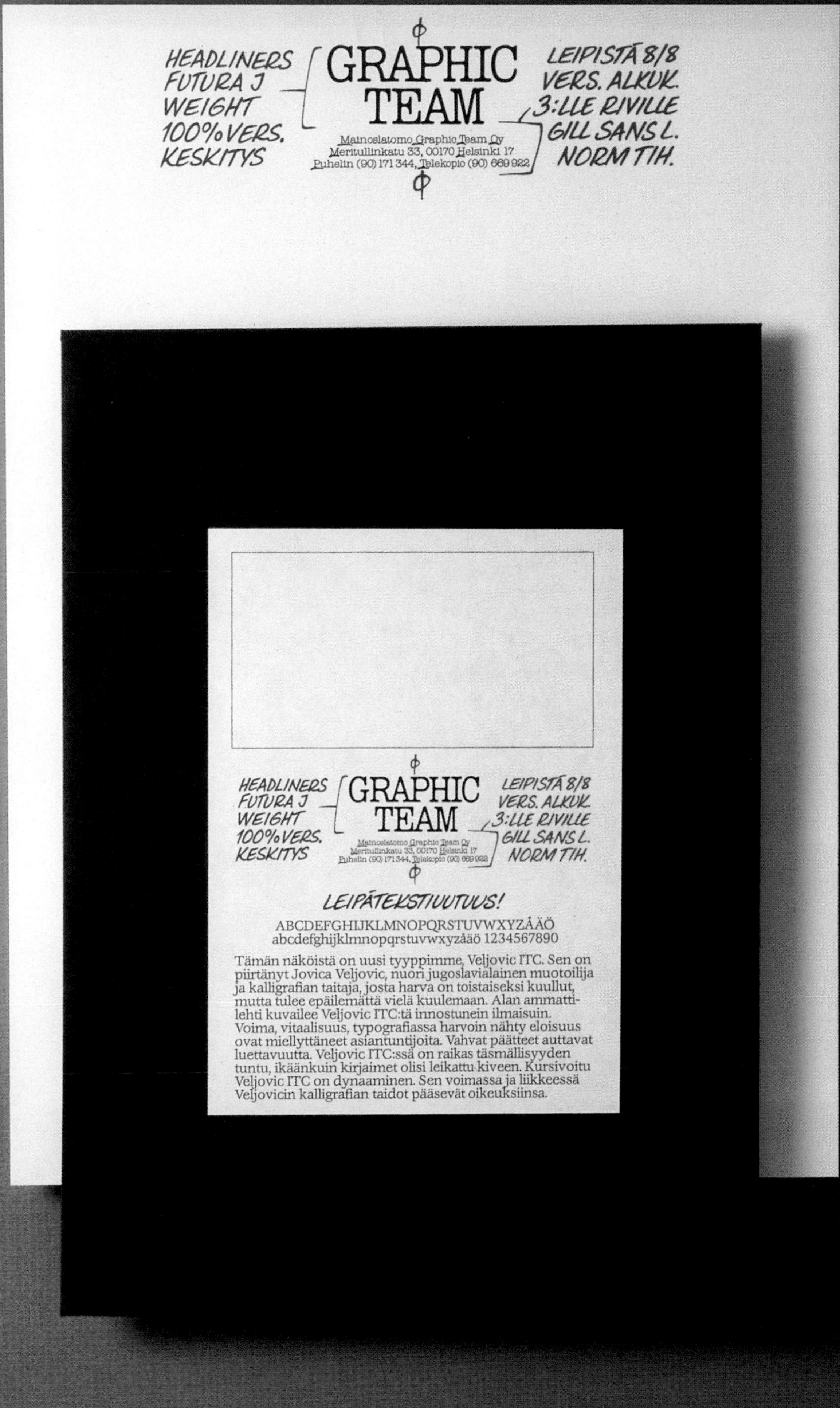

HEADLINERS
FUTURA J
WEIGHT
100% VERS.
KESKITYS

GRAPHIC TEAM

Mainostatomo Graphic Team Oy
Meritullinkatu 33, 00170 Helsinki 17
Puhelin (90) 171 344, Telekopio (90) 669 922

LEIPISTÄ 8/8
VERS. ALKUK.
3:LLE RIVILLE
GILL SANS L.
NORM TIH.

HEADLINERS
FUTURA J
WEIGHT
100% VERS.
KESKITYS

GRAPHIC TEAM

Mainostatomo Graphic Team Oy
Meritullinkatu 33, 00170 Helsinki 17
Puhelin (90) 171 344, Telekopio (90) 669 922

LEIPISTÄ 8/8
VERS. ALKUK.
3:LLE RIVILLE
GILL SANS L.
NORM TIH.

LEIPÄTEKSTIUUTUUS!

ABCDEFGHIJKLMNOPQRSTUVWXYZÅÄÖ
abcdefghijklmnopqrstuvwxyzåäö 1234567890

Tämän näköistä on uusi tyyppimme, Veljovic ITC. Sen on
piirtänyt Jovica Veljovic, nuori jugoslavialainen muotoilija
ja kalligrafian taitaja, josta harva on toistaiseksi kuullut,
mutta tulee epäilemättä vielä kuulemaan. Alan ammatti-
lehti kuvailee Veljovic ITC:tä innostunein ilmaisuin.
Voima, vitaalisuus, typografiassa harvoin nähty eloisuus
ovat miellyttäneet asiantuntijoita. Vahvat päätteet auttavat
luettavuutta. Veljovic ITC:ssä on raikas täsmällisyyden
tuntu, ikäänkuin kirjaimet olisi leikattu kiveen. Kursivoitu
Veljovic ITC on dynaaminen. Sen voimassa ja liikkeessä
Veljovicin kalligrafian taidot pääsevät oikeuksiinsa.

Client: Lizabeth Kelly Lyles
Design Firm: Lizabeth Kelly Lyles Graphics/Illustration
Designer: Lizabeth Kelly Lyles
Art Director: Lizabeth Kelly Lyles
Paper/Printing: Four colors on 24-lb. Strathmore Bright White Laid

LIZABETH KELLY LYLES
GRAPHICS / ILLUSTRATION
638 W. Emerson
Seattle, WA 98119
(206) 283-6399

LIZABETH KELLY LYLES
GRAPHICS / ILLUSTRATION
638 W. Emerson
Seattle, WA 98119
(206) 283-6399

LIZABETH KELLY LYLES
GRAPHICS / ILLUSTRATION
638 W. Emerson
Seattle, WA 98119
(206) 283-6399

Client: Carlson Ferrin Architects

Design Firm: Hornall Anderson Design Works

Designer: Jack Anderson

Art Director: Jack Anderson

CARLSON/FERRIN

A R C H I T E C T S

CARLSON/FERRIN

A R C H I T E C T S

☐   ☐

TRANSMITTAL   MEMORANDUM

CARLSON/FERRIN

A R C H I T E C T S

We are sending
you the following:

☐ Attached

☐ Prints

☐ Submittal

☐ Under Separate Cover

☐ Originals

☐ Samples

☐ _____

1925
Post Alley
Seattle, WA
98101

For Your:

☐ Information and Use

☐ Preview and Comment

☐ As Requested

Action Required:

☐ As Indicated

☐ No Action Required

☐ For Signature & Return

CARLSON/FERRIN

A R C H I T E C T S

206/
441-3066

1928
Pike Place Market
Seattle, WA
98101

Diane Jacobsen

3rd Floor
Champion Bldg.

If enclosures are not as noted
kindly notify us at once.

By: _____

cc: _____

1928
Pike Place Market
Seattle, WA
98101
206/441-3066

OSAMA SCRITTURA SPA

Armando Tschang
Amministratore unico

Via 1º Maggio, 11 20060 Mombretto di Mediglia (Milano) Telefono 02.9067292/3 - 9067652/3 Telefax. 02.9067665

BARRACLOUGHS

G. Barraclough Ltd, Swaledale House, West Yorkshire Industrial Estate, Toftshaw Lane, Bradford, West Yorkshire BD4 8SX.

Tel: 0274 684772 Fax: 0274 681088 Telex: 517676. Reg Office: King William House, Market Place, Hull, Reg No. 2295092 England.

HOT SPOT
Pohjoinen Hesperiankatu 5 A 14,
00260 Helsinki, puh. (90) 490 349.
Paakki KOP Aleksanterinkatu 163110-2017729

OPERNHAUS ZÜRICH

FALKENSTRASSE 1   CH-8008 ZÜRICH
TELEFON 01 / 251 69 20   TELEX 815 988 OHZ CH

Client: Hot Spot
Design Firm: Jukka Veistola
Designer: Jukka Veistola
Art Director: Jukka Veistola
Paper/Printing: Three colors

Client: Opera House Zurich
Design Firm: Geissbuhler AGI
Designer: K.D. Geissbuhler
Art Director: K.D. Geissbuhler
Paper/Printing: Two colors on smooth, bright white bond

Client: Identity program for Susan Kurtzman/Creative Writing
Design Firm: Ruenitz & Co.
Designer: George Ruenitz
Art Director: Gloria Ruenitz
Paper/Printing: Three colors on 24-lb. Strathmore Writing Wove

SUSAN KURTZMAN

CREATIVE WRITING

Direct Marketing
Advertising
Editorial

23 Fairfield Avenue   Westport, Connecticut 06880   Telephone 203-227-5580

Client: Esse Editrice s.r.l.
Design Firm: Visual Due Studio
Designer: Vittorio Prina
Art Director: Vittorio Prina

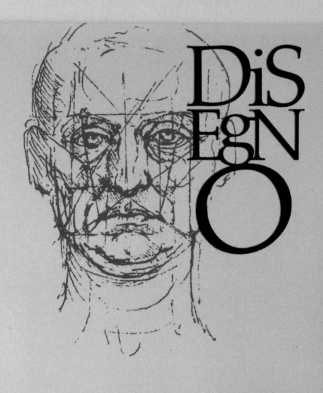

Rivista di Tecnica e Creatività

Roberto Salardi
Direttore Responsabile

Rivista di Tecnica e Creatività ESSE s.r.l. Viale Renato Serra, 14 20148 Milano Italia Tel. 02.3270337

Client: MD Orthotic & Prosthetic Laboratory, Inc.
Design Firm: Gerhardt & Clemons, Inc.
Designer: Beth Nagy
Art Director: Kristie J. Clemons
Paper/Printing: Two colors on Speckletone Ivory White Text

Client: Peter Crockett
Designer: Peter Crockett
Art Director: Peter Crockett
Paper/Printing: Two colors plus opaque white on Speckletone Kraft

Client: Chironet, Inc.
Design Firm: Muller + Company
Designer: Patrice Eilts
Art Director: Patrice Eilts
Paper/Printing: Two colors on Neenah Classic Laid

Client: David Westwood & Associates
Design Firm: David Westwood & Associates
Designer: David Westwood
Art Director: David Westwood
Paper/Printing: Cool gray and yellow inks on Fox River Qnionskin

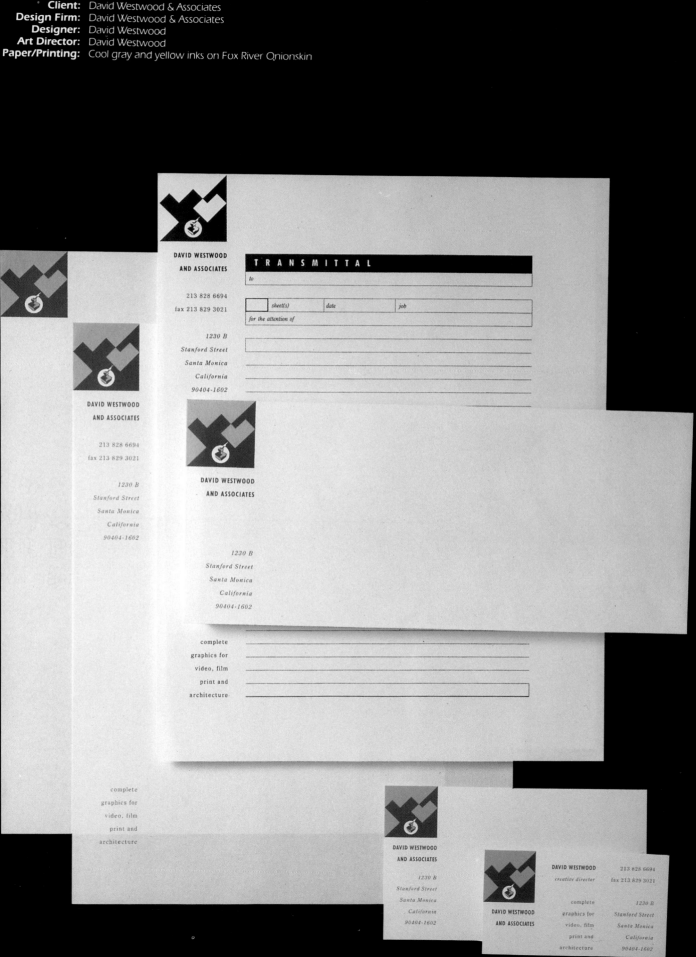

Client: Henson Design Associates
Design Firm: Henson Design Associates
Designer: Chip Henson
Art Director: Julie Henson
Paper/Printing: Two colors on Classic Crest/Avon Brilliant White

HENSON

4102 East

Ray Road,

Suite 1170

DESIGN

Phoenix,

Arizona

85044

ASSOCIATES

602.759.5325

Julie Henson

HENSON

4102 East

Ray Road,

Suite 1170

DESIGN

Phoenix,

Arizona

85044

ASSOCIATES

602.759.5325

Client: Schreibman Creative Services
Design Firm: Katherine DeVault Design
Designer: Katherine DeVault

SCHREIBMAN CREATIVE SERVICES

1102 17th Avenue S. • Suite 200 • Nashville, TN 37212

A few words from SCHREIBMAN CREATIVE SERVICES

CREATIVE THAT WORKS ACROSS THE BOARD

1102 17th Avenue S. • Suite 200 • Nashville, TN 37212 • (615) 321-3512

Client: Narrow Road Music Ministry
Design Firm: Hugh Dunnahoe Illustration & Design
Designer: Hugh Dunnahoe
Art Director: Hugh Dunnahoe
Paper/Printing: Two colors on Classic Crest Natural White

Client: Fotostudio Robert Schilder
Design Firm: Vorm Vijf Grafisch Ontwerpteam
Designer: Eric van Casteren
Art Director: Eric van Casteren
Paper/Printing: Four colors

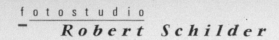

fotostudio
Robert Schilder

1/250

1/125

1/60

1/30

1/15

1/8

1/4

1/2

0

1

2

4

8

90   64   45   32   22   16   11   8   5.6

Stuiverstraat 1

5611 TA Eindhoven

(040) 110 210

K.v.K. nr. 42092

Rabobank Eindhoven Nrd. 17 82 38 856

Leveringen volgens de voorwaarden zoals gedeponeerd bij de Kamer van Koophandel

Client: Jim McColl Associates
Design Firm: McIlroy Coates
Designer: Ian McIlroy
Art Director: Ian McIlroy
Paper/Printing: Two colors on 100 gsm Conqueror Wove

JIM McCOLL ASSOCIATES

CONSULTING CIVIL
AND
STRUCTURAL ENGINEERS

56 CONSTITUTION STREET
LEITH, EDINBURGH EH6 6RS
TEL: 031-555 0721
FAX: 031-555 0723

PRINCIPAL
JIM McCOLL BSc CEng MICE FI Struct E

Client: Lion Distribution s.p.A.
Design Firm: Visual Due Studio
Designer: Vittorio Prina
Art Director: Vittorio Prina

Client: The Goddard Manton Partnership
Design Firm: John Nash & Friends
Designer: John Nash
Art Director: Jonn Nash
Paper/Printing: Four colors

The Goddard Manton Partnership
ARCHITECTS

Anthony Goddard
ARCHITECT

The Goddard Manton Partnership
67 George Row London SE16 4UH Tel. 01-237 2016
Facsimile 01-237 7850

Don Manton
ARCHITECT

The Goddard Manton Partnership
67 George Row London SE16 4UH Tel. 01-237 2016
Facsimile 01-237 7850

67 GEORGE ROW LONDON SE16 4UH TELEPHONE 01-237 2016 FACSIMILE 01-237 7850

VAT NO. 241 4572 79

Client: Janis Boehm Design
Design Firm: Janis Boehm Design
Designers: Janis Boehm, Tracy Gibbons
Art Director: Janis Boehm
Paper/Printing: Black ink, blind embossed sculptured die

Client: Textilion Ltd.
Design Firm: Royle-Murgatroyd Design Associates Ltd.
Designers: Royle-Murgatroyd Design Associates Ltd.
Art Director: Keith Murgatroyd
Paper/Printing: Two colors, embossed, on Strathmore Bright White Woven

Textilion

Textilion Limited
Newcastle Division:
Norham Road North
North Shields
Tyne & Wear NE29 8RZ
Tel: 091-257 0181
Fax: 091-259 2224
Telex: 537736

Textilion
PRESS ▼ RELEASE
Telephone: 0533 762621

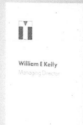

William E Kelly
Managing Director

Textilion

Textilion Limited
Newcastle Division:
Norham Road North
North Shields
Tyne & Wear NE29 8RZ
Tel: 091-257 0181
Fax: 091-259 2224
Telex: 537736

Directors: P T S Boyd, W Kelly,
N Bostock, R Winckles (NON EXECUTIVE).

Registered Office:
23-37 Spalding Street, Leicester LE5 4PL
Registered in England No. 2320230

Textilion Limited
Head Office: 23-37 Spalding Street, Leicester LE5 4PL   Tel: 0533 762621   Fax: 0533 741594   Telex: 341408

Client: Rickabaugh Graphics
Design Firm: Rickabaugh Graphics
Designer: Eric Rickabaugh
Art Director: Eric Rickabaugh
Paper/Printing: Two colors on Protocol Writing

Client: Smash Advertising
Design Firm: Corey McPherson Nash
Designer: Scott Nash
Art Director: Scott Nash
Paper/Printing: Two colors on Strathmore Writing White

Client: Franz Moore Studio
Design Firm: Marks/Bielenberg Design
Designer: John Bielenberg
Art Director: John Bielenberg
Paper/Printing: Two colors plus pearlescent gray foil on Simpson Starwhite Vicksburg

FRANZ-MOORE STUDIO

421 TEHAMA

SAN FRANCISCO, CA 94103

TEL 415-495-6421

FRANZ-MOORE STUDIO

421 TEHAMA

SAN FRANCISCO, CA 94103

TEL 415-495-6421

PAUL FRANZ-MOORE

FRANZ-MOORE STUDIO

421 TEHAMA

SAN FRANCISCO, CA 94103

TEL 415-495-6421

Client: Enterprise Media
Design Firm: Corey McPherson Nash
Designer: Joanna Bodenweber, Scott Nash
Art Director: Scott Nash
Paper/Printing: Three colors on Strathmore Writing White

Enterprise Media Inc.

Janet L. Goff
Vice President, Sales and Marketing

374 Congress St.
Suite 400
Boston, Massachusetts 02210
617·482·5001

Client: Minagawa Artlines
Design Firm: Julie Losch Design
Designer: Julie Losch
Art Director: Julie Losch
Paper/Printing: Two colors on Strathmore Bright White Wove

Client: CAR
Design Firm: Vorm Vijf Grafisch Ontwerpteam
Designer: Bart de Groot
Art Director: Bart de Groot
Paper/Printing: Two colors on Gemeente Rotterdam

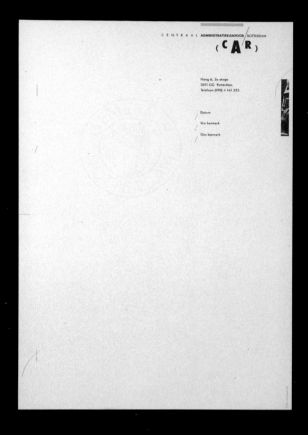

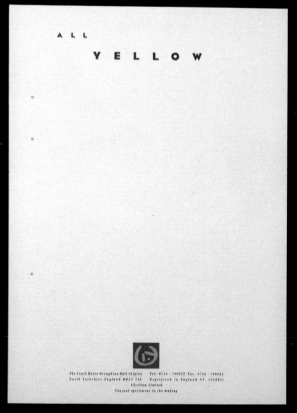

Client: Management Dynamics, Inc.
Design Firm: The Corporate Communications Group/
Mirenbury & Company
Designers: Barry L. Mirenburg
Art Director: Barry L. Mirenburg
Paper/Printing: One color on 24-lb. Classic Crest Bright White

Client: All Yellow Sportswear Limited
Design Firm: Elmwood Design Limited
Designers: Clare Walker
Art Director: Clare Walker
Paper/Printing: Three colors on Strathmore Esprit Bright White

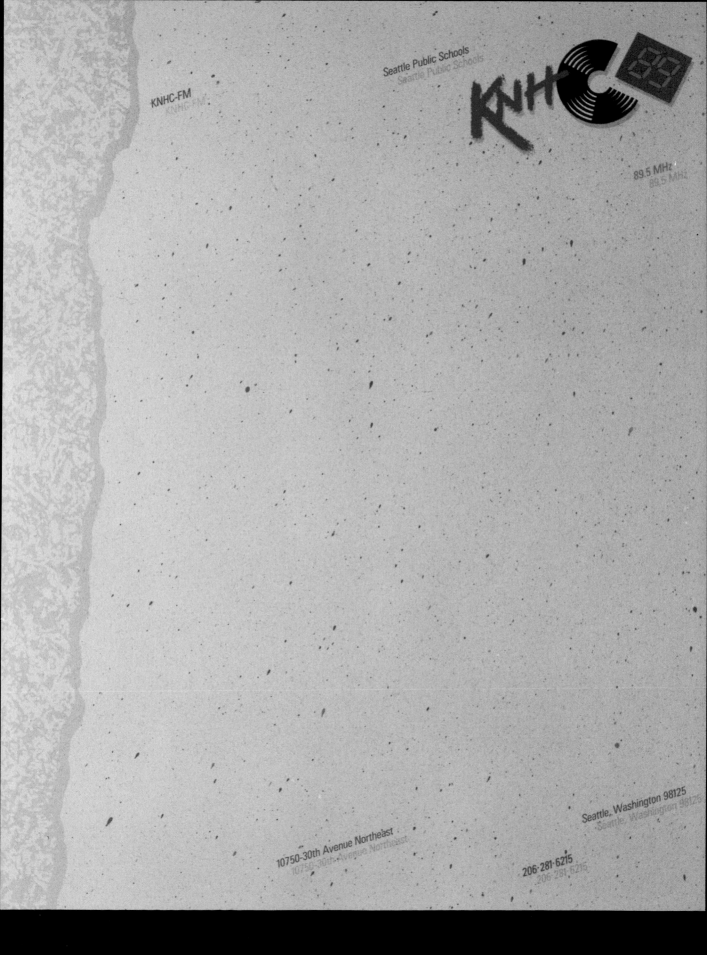

KNHC-FM

Seattle Public Schools

89.5 MHz

10750-30th Avenue Northeast

Seattle, Washington 98125

206-281-6215

Client: Arthur Jack Snyder
Design Firm: Richardson or Richardson
Designer: Diane Gilleland
Art Director: Forrest Richardson
Paper/Printing: Stationery: Two colors on 24-lb. Protocol 100;
Business Card: Two colors on cover stock

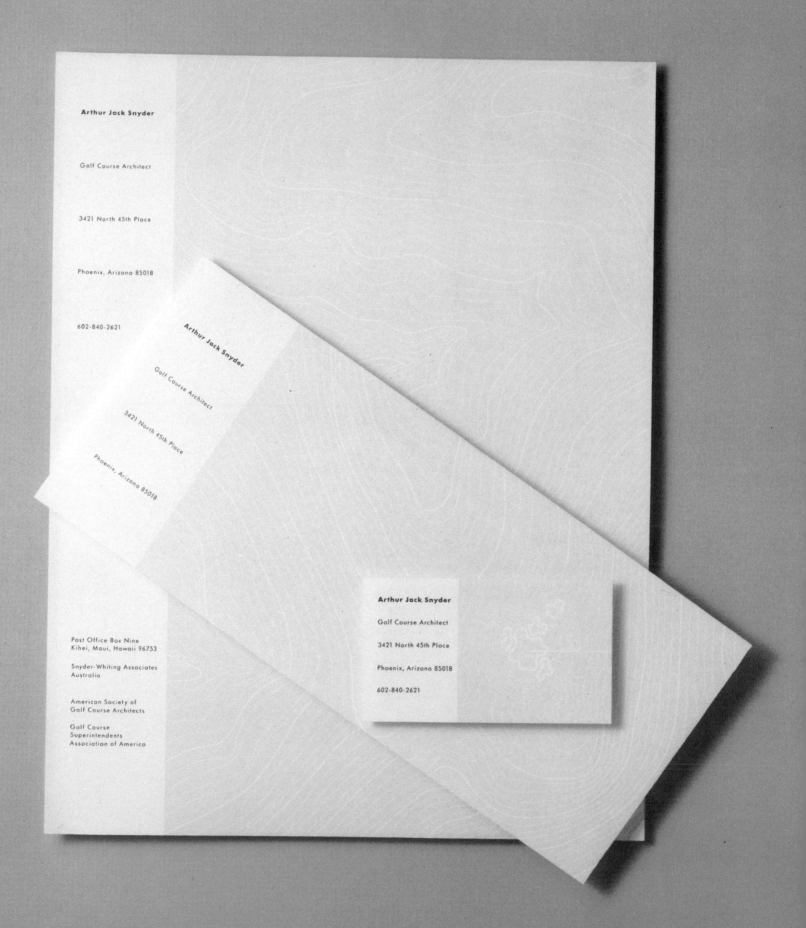

Client: Signage Resource Consultants
Design Firm: Hugh Dunnahoe Illustration & Design
Designer: Hugh Dunnahoe
Art Director: Hugh Dunnahoe
Paper/Printing: Four colors on Curtis Brightwater Bright

Client: Approach
Design Firm: Hornall Anderson Design Works
Designers: Jack Anderson, Juliet Shen
Art Director: Jack Anderson

A P P R O A C H

Translating
Visions
Into
Strategies

711 N 86th St.
Seattle, WA
98103
206 783-6033

Designer: Richard Leeds
Art Director: Richard Leeds
Paper/Printing: Four colors on 24-lb. Protocol Bright White Wove

2995

WOODSIDE

ROAD

SUITE 400

WOODSIDE

CA 94062

MURALS
TROMPE L'OEIL
DESIGN
FAUX FINISH

LINDA FEALK-HOFFMAN 415 324-0323
2995 WOODSIDE ROAD, SUITE 400, WOODSIDE, CA 94062

2995 WOODSIDE ROAD, SUITE 400, WOODSIDE, CA 94062 **415 324-0323**

Client: R&R, Rob Tunkin
Design Firm: They Design
Designer: Guido Brouwers
Paper/Printing: Two colors on Strathmore White Wove

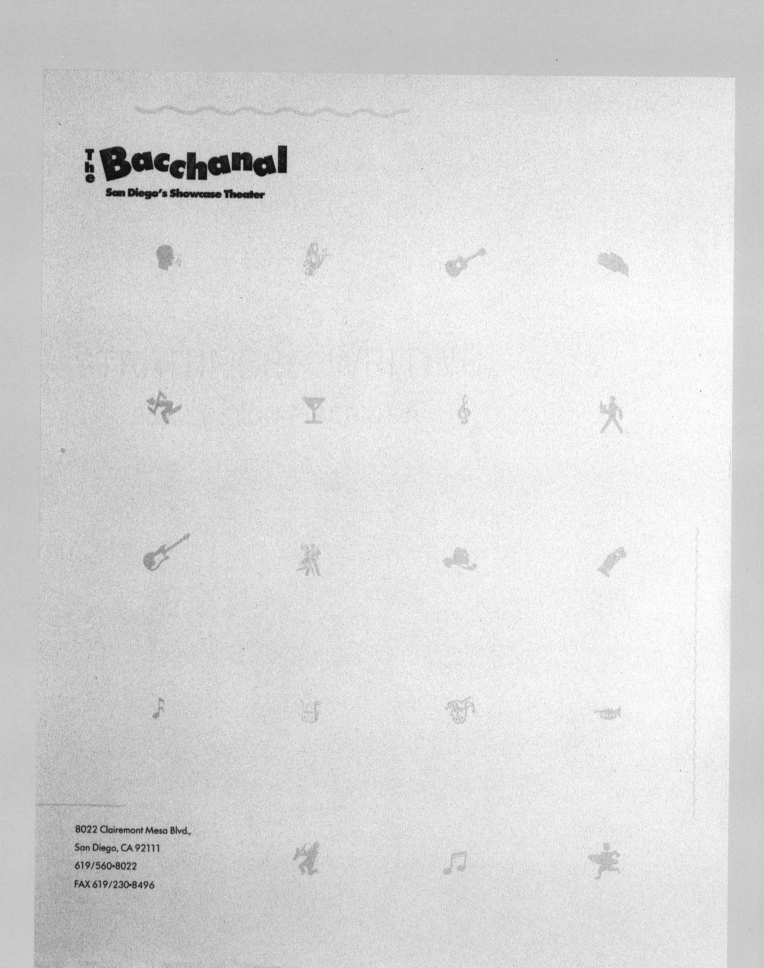

Client: Mary Atols & John Hoffman, agents
Design Firm: Barnes Design Office
Designer: Jeff A. Barnes
Art Director: Jeff A. Barnes
Paper/Printing: One color on Suecia Antiqua Gray

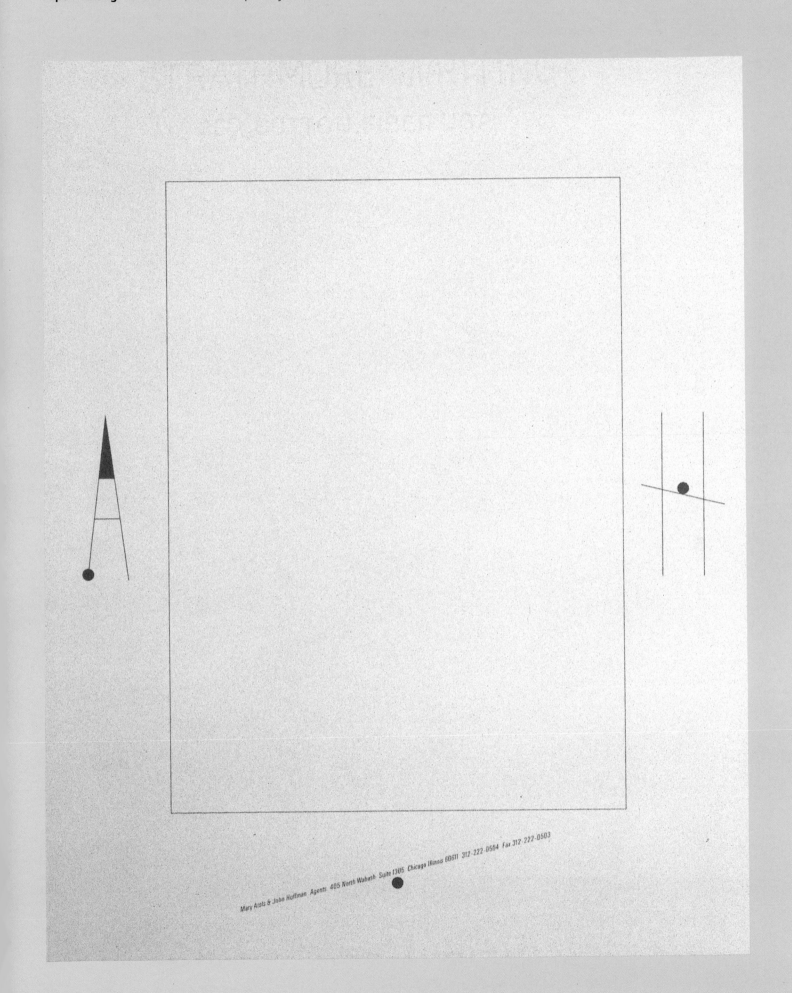

Mary Atols & John Hoffman, Agents 405 North Wabash Suite 1305 Chicago Illinois 60611 312-222-0564 Fax 312-222-0503

Design Firm: Bullet Communications
Designer: Tim Scott
Art Director: Tim Scott
Paper/Printing: Two colors on 70-lb. Beckett Ridge White Book

BULLET COMMUNICATIONS™
666 W. OAKDALE AVE. CHICAGO, IL 60657 TELE: 312 327 6662

P R E M O N T • S N C
Via Levate, 57 24044 Dalmine (Bergamo) Telefono 035. 562735

P R E M O N T • S N C

P R E M O N T • S N C
di Carla e Isabella Benedetti Premontaggio, montaggio, typonaggio Via Levate, 57 24044 Dalmine (BG) Tel. 035. 562735 C.F./P. IVA 01806560163 CCIAA BG 238403

Client: Roger Paperno Photography
Design Firm: Lisa Levin Design
Designer: Lisa Levin
Art Director: Lisa Levin
Paper/Printing: Three colors on 24-lb. Simpson Protocol Writing Bright White

Client: The Communiqué Group
Design Firm: Ruby Shoes Studio
Designer: Karen Watkins
Art Director: Susan Tyrrell
Paper/Printing: Two colors plus emboss on Cranes Bright White Wove

Advertising
Marketing
Promotions

42 Glen Avenue
Newton Centre, MA 02159

617-527-2230

Advertising
Marketing
Promotions

42 Glen Avenue
Newton Centre, MA 02159

Advertising, Marketing, Promotions

42 Glen Avenue
Newton Centre, MA 02159
617-527-2230

James H. Kurland
President

Accent on excellence.

Client: Danilee Pty. Ltd.
Design Firm: Raymond Bennett Design Pty. Ltd.
Designer: Raymond Bennett
Art Director: Raymond Bennett
Paper/Printing: Two colors on Chartham Mill White Laid

Client: Bob Orr/Organizational Team Building
Design Firm: The Bradford Lawton Design Group
Designer: Bradford Lawton
Art Directors: Bradford Lawton, Scott Creamer
Paper/Printing: Two colors on Protocol Bright White Wove

ORGANIZATIONAL
TEAM BUILDING

ORGANIZATIONAL
TEAM BUILDING

117 WEST CRAIG PLACE
SAN ANTONIO, TEXAS 78212
(512) 734-7323

117 WEST CRAIG PLACE
SAN ANTONIO, TEXAS 78212
(512) 734-7323

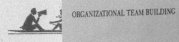

ORGANIZATIONAL TEAM BUILDING

Client: Huntington Bank
Design Firm: Rickabaugh Graphics
Designer: Eric Rickabaugh
Art Director: Eric Rickabaugh
Paper/Printing: Four colors

Client: The Design Company
Design Firm: The Design Company
Designer: Marcia Romanuck
Art Director: Marcia Romanuck
Paper/Printing: Two colors on Weston Whisper White

THE DESIGN COMPANY / BOSTON
15 Sleeper Street • Suite 502 • Boston, MA 02210 • (617) 338-0974 • FAX (617) 338-1674

Client: Cranmer Art Conservation
Design Firm: Julie Losch Design
Designer: Julie Losch
Paper/Printing: Six colors on 24-lb. Cranes Crest Fluorescent White

CRANMER
A R T C O N S E R V A T I O N

CRANMER
A R T C O N S E R V A T I O N

Invoice

21 Mercer Street
New York, N.Y. 10013
212 966-9167

21 Mercer Street
New York, N.Y. 10013
212 966-9167

21 Mercer Street
New York, N.Y. 10013

CRANMER
A R T C O N S E R V A T I O N

CRANMER
A R T C O N S E R V A T I O N

21 Mercer Street
New York, N.Y. 10013
212 966-9167

Dana Cranmer

Client: Children's Media Lab
Design Firm: Rene Yung Communications Design
Designer: Rene Yung
Art Director: Rene Yung

Client: Tandem Design
Design Firm: Tandem Design
Art Directors: Stephan Donche, Theresa Vandenberg
Paper/Printing: Two colors

Client: Frank Simon/Simon Photographic
Designer: Margo Halverson-Heywood
Paper/Printing: Two colors and five percent screen tint on 70-lb. Beckett Enhance Text

Client: HM Graphics
Design Firm: Frankenberry, Laughlin & Constable, Inc.
Designer: Mark Kuerner
Art Director: Mark Kuerner
Paper/Printing: Seven colors on French Speckletone

Client: John Nash & Friends
Design Firm: John Nash & Friends
Designer: John Nash
Art Director: John Nash
Paper/Printing: Two colors

JOHN NASH & FRIENDS

Graphic Design Consultants

10 New Concordia Wharf Mill Street London SE1 2BA Telephone 01-231 9161 Fax 01-237 3719

John Nash FCSD

John Nash & Friends
Graphic Design Consultants

10 New Concordia Wharf
Mill Street
London SE1 2BA

Telephone 01-231 9161
Fax 01-237 3719

John Nash & Friends Limited Registered in England No. 1125018 Registered office 10 New Concordia Wharf Mill Street London SE1 2BA

Client: Grand Canyon Railway
Design Firm: Morgan & Company
Designer: Roland Dahlquist
Illustrator: Roland Dahlquist
Art Directors: Margo Halverson-Heywood, David C. Morgan
Paper/Printing: Stationery & Envelope: One color on 70-lb. French Speckletone Text Creme;
Business Card: Four colors on 80-lb. Cover

4350 East Camelback Road
Suite 100B
Phoenix, Arizona 85018
602/956-3393

Client: Ka Cheong Antique
Design Firm: Alan Chan Design Co.
Designers: Alan Chan, Phillip Leung, Andy Ip
Art Director: Alan Chan

家昌　香港荷李活道十三號地下　13, Hollywood Road, G/F., Hong Kong. Telephone: 5-8451508

KA CHEONG
antique

Telephone: 5-8451508
13, Hollywood Road, G/F., Hong Kong,
香港荷李活道十三號地下
家昌

KA CHEONG
antique

陳昌貞
Beatrice Chan

KA CHEONG
antique

家昌
香港荷李活道十三號地下
13, Hollywood Rd., G/F.,
Hong Kong.
Telephone: 5-8451508

169

Client: Offis, Office for Innovation Services
Design Firm: Vorm Vijf Grafisch Ontwerpteam BNO
Designer: Bart de Groot
Art Director: Bart de Groot
Paper/Printing: Four colors

Client: Artocean Aquarium Engineering Ltd.
Design Firm: Kan Tai-Keung Design & Associates Ltd.
Designer: Kan Tai-keung
Art Director: Kan Tai-keung

富洋水族工程有限公司
Artocean Aquarium Engineering Ltd.
186-188 Lockhart Road, Wanchai, Hong Kong
Tel: 5-732692 Telex: 54427 ONTCO HX

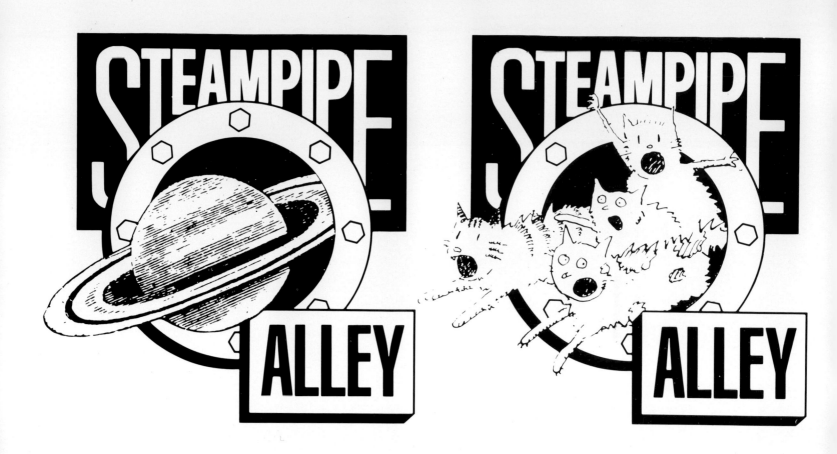

Client: Steampipe Alley Television
Design Firm: Corey McPherson Nash
Designers: Scott Nash, Kyoko Tanaka
Art Director: Scott Nash

Client: Ranchos Dos Canadas
Design Firm: Knoth & Meads
Designer: Jose Serrano
Art Director: Jose Serrano

RANCHO DOS CAÑADAS

RAGÚ

CREATIVE & PACKAGE DESIGN

SAN FRANCISCO
LANDSCAPE GARDEN
SHOW

Client: Ragú
Design Firm: Hornall Anderson Design Works
Designer: Jack Anderson
Art Director: Jack Anderson

Client: Washington State
Design Firm: Port Miolla Associates, Inc.
Designer: Port Miolla Associates
Art Director: Port Miolla Associates

Client: San Francisco Parks
Design Firm: Thompson Design Group
Designers: Dennis Thompson, Elizabeth Berta
Art Directors: Dennis Thompson
Jody Thompson

Client: N.Y. City Sports Commission
Design Firm: DeSola Group
Designer: DeSola Group
Art Director: DeSola Group

1787-1987
WASHINGTON
CELEBRATES
THE
CONSTITUTION

NEW YORK CITY
SPORTS
COMMISSION

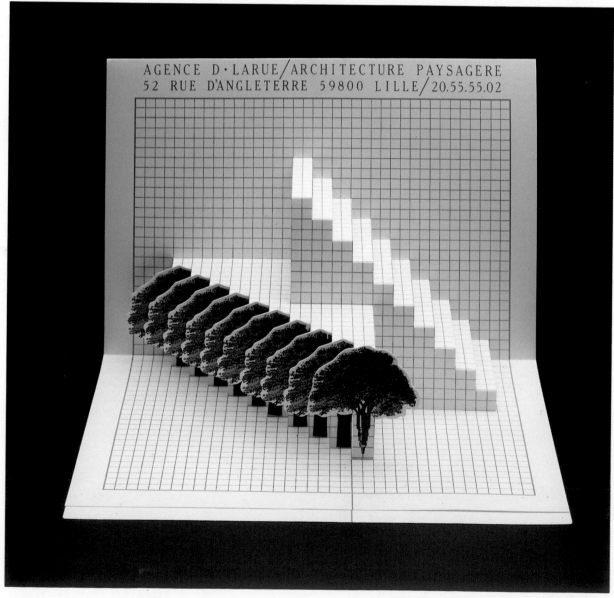

Client: Agence D'Laure/Architecture
Design Firm: Vezinhet
Designer: Vezinhet

Client: Andresen Typographics
Design Firm: Bright & Associates
Designer: Wilson Ong
Art Director: Keith Bright
Paper/Printing: One color on Cranes Crest

Client: Mors
Design Firm: Samenwerkende Ontwerpers
Designer: André Toet
Art Director: André Toet

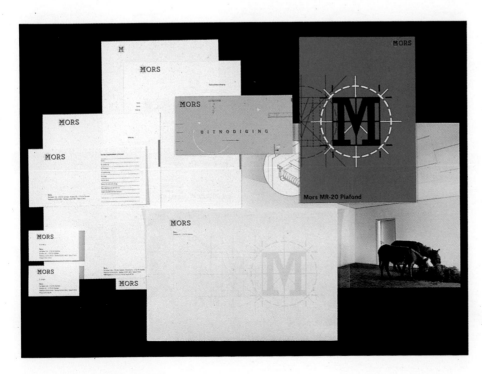

Client: Sunset Cliffs Wash & Dry
Design Firm: They Design
Designer: Guido Brouwers
Art Director: Guido Brouwers

Client: The October Group
Design Firm: David Westwood & Associates
Designer: David Westwood
Art Director: David Westwood

Client: Rob Tonian/Iguanas Restaurant
Design Firm: They Design
Designer: Guido Brouwers
Art Director: Guido Brouwers

THE OCTOBER GROUP

IGUANAS

DUNKLEY & COMPANY

THE CREATIVE FLORAL DESIGN GROUP

Client: Dunkley & Company
Design Firm: Carter Wong Limited
Designer: Alison Tomlin
Art Directors: Alison Tomlin, Phil Carter

DOUBLE EAGLE

Client: Double Eagle Lodge
Design Firm: The Weller Institute for the Cure of Design, Inc.
Designer: Don Weller
Art Director: Don Weller

Client: Information Associates, Inc.
Design Firm: Conge Design
Designers: Bob Conge, Robin Banker
Art Directors: Bob Conge, Steve Roberts

CIRCLE OF SUPPORT℠

Client: Haberlach
Design Firm: Rubin Cordaro Design
Designer: John Haines
Art Director: Bruce Rubin
Paper/Printing: Strathmore 24-lb. Writing Bright White Wove

Haberlach

Haberlach

Interiors

Haberlach, Inc.
165 North
Western Avenue
Saint Paul,
MN 55102

Haberlach

Interiors

Haberlach, Inc.
165 North
Western Avenue
Saint Paul,
MN 55102
612 292 9793

Rita Wayne
Allied Member ASID

Interiors

Haberlach, Inc.
165 North
Western Avenue
Saint Paul,
MN 55102
612 292 9793

Client: Akagi Design
Design Firm: Akagi Design
Designer: Doug Akagi
Art Director: Doug Akagi
Paper/Printing: Stationery: Three colors on 24-lb. Cranes Crest Opaque Wove Fluorescent;
Business Card: Three colors on 12-pt. Kromekote 2S

Client: Lewis And Clark
Design Firm: Ruby Shoes Studio, Inc.
Designer: Jane Lee
Art Director: Susan Tyrrell
Paper/Printing: Two colors on Strathmore Bright White Wove

**LEWIS
AND
CLARK**

We Discover

Equipment

Opportunities

**LEWIS
AND
CLARK**

*We Discover
Equipment
Opportunities*

Beth Lewis

*Distributors of Previously-Owned
Test and Manufacturing Equipment*

P.O. Box 665, Boston, MA 02258   *(617) 926-8338*

**LEWIS
AND
CLARK**

*We Discover
Equipment
Opportunities*

P.O. Box 665, Boston, Massachusetts 02258

LEWIS & CLARK, inc., P.O. Box 665, Boston, Massachusetts 02258   *(617) 926-8338*   *Fax: (617) 923-0633*

Client: The Exercise Center
Design Firm: Debra Malinics Advertising
Designer: Debra Malinics
Art Director: Debra Malinics
Paper/Printing: Two colors on Strathmore White

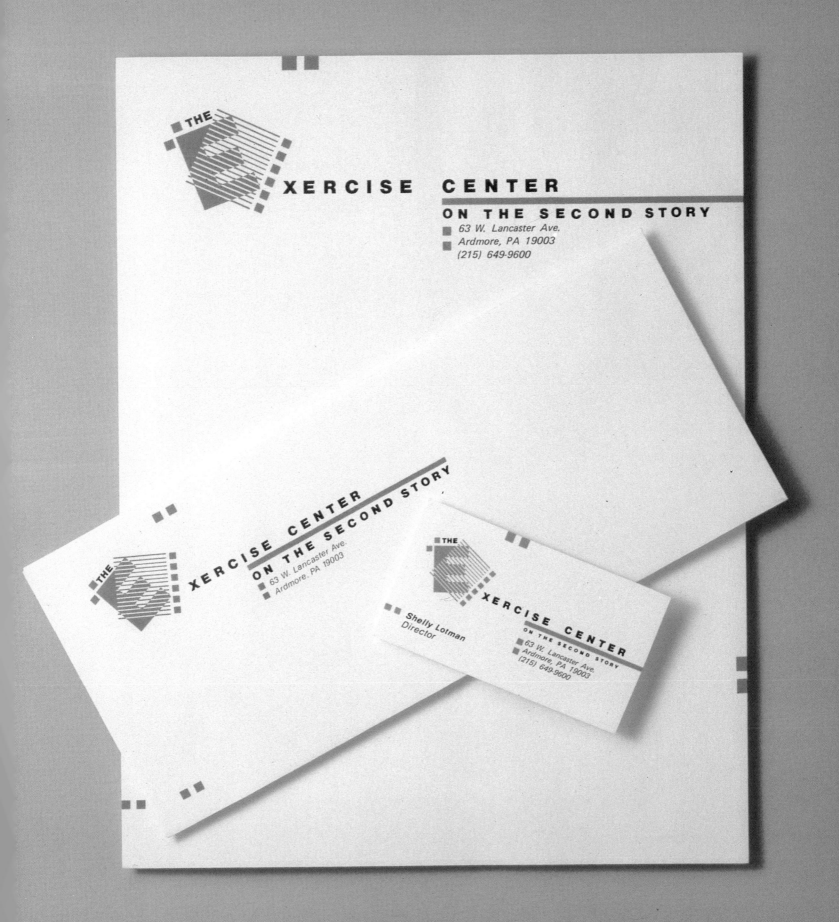

Bemiddelings- en coördinatieburo
Onroerend goed, hypotheken en verzekeringen

Deylerweg 144
2241 AK Wassenaar
Telefoon/fax (01751) 1 90 66
Postbank 509292

amica

Wassenaar

betreft

uw kenmerk
ons kenmerk

Deylerweg 144
2241 AK Wassenaar
Telefoon/fax (01751) 1 90 66

amica

Handelsregister 's Gravenhage
nummer 120265

Deylerweg 144
2241 AK Wassenaar
Telefoon/fax (01751) 1 90 66

amica

Rob L.M.G. van Gestel

Bemiddelings- en coördinatieburo
Onroerend goed, hypotheken en verzekeringen

THE LIVELY MIND

Jody Potts, Ph.D.

THE LIVELY MIND

6124 Sherry Lane, #146

Dallas, Texas 75225

THE LIVELY MIND   *Jody Potts, Ph.D.*

6124 Sherry Lane, #146

Dallas, Texas 75225

214·363·1621

Seminars for thinking better, working smarter   THE LIVELY MIND

6124 Sherry Lane, #146   Dallas, Texas 75225   214·363·1621

Client: Beth Israel Medical Center, Food & Nutrition Services
Design Firm: Shapiro Design Associates Inc.
Designers: Donald Burg, Ellen Shapiro
Art Director: Ellen Shapiro
Illustrator: Susan Stillman

Client: The Paradigm Corporation
Designer: Peter Crockett
Art Director: Peter Crockett
Paper/Printing: Two colors on Strathmore Writing

The Paradigm Corporation

Suite 290
9 Monroe Parkway
Lake Oswego, Oregon 97034

503·636·7559

The Paradigm Corporation

Suite 290   9 Monroe Parkway   Lake Oswego, Oregon 97034   503·636·7559

Client: Ellen Wingard
Design Firm: Ruby Shoes Studio
Designer: Jane Lee
Art Director: Susan Tyrrell
Paper/Printing: Two color with halftone screen printed on Strathmore Bright White Woven stock

Client: Altmann Construction, inc.
Design Firm: Cahan & Associates
Designer: Erik Adigard
Art Director: Bill Cahan
Paper/Printing: Two colors on Starwhite Vicksburg Text, Tiara White, vellum finish

High

Performance

Health

Ellen S. Wingard

28 Orchard Street

Wellesley, MA 02181

(617) 237-5431

Altmann Construction, Inc.

228 RAILROAD AVE · DANVILLE, CA 94526 · 415.837.2847

MIDSTATES
AUTO REPS INC.

114 N.W. 5th Street
Suite 293
Ankeny, Iowa 50021
515.964.9545

CHARACTERS & Color

619 South La Brea Avenue
Los Angeles, California 90036
(213) 938-3668

Client: Midstates Auto Reps
Design Firm: Mauck + Associates
Designer: Kent Mauck
Art Director: Kent Mauck
Paper/Printing: Two colors, embossed, on Strathmore Bright White Woven stock

Client: Characters & Color
Design Firm: Stan Evenson Design
Designer: Stan Evenson
Art Director: Stan Evenson
Paper/Printing: Three colors on Cranes Crest

Client: Estes Company
Design Firm: Boelts Bros. Design Inc.
Designers: Jackson Boelts, Eric Boelts
Paper/Printing: Four colors on 70-lb. Curtis Brightwater Text

THE ARBORETUM

E X C L U S I V E · A P A R T M E N T · L I V I N G

4700 North Kolb Road · Tucson · Arizona · 85715 · (602) 299-8200

Client: Julie Losch Design
Design Firm: Julie Losch Design
Designer: Julie Losch
Paper/Printing: Four colors on Strathmore 24-lb. Writing Bright White Wove

Client: Margo Halverson-Heywood
Design Firm: Scintilla Press
Designer: Margo Halverson-Heywood
Paper/Printing: Two colors on 24-lb. Classic Crest Writing

Graphic Designer
2005 South La Corta Drive
Tempe Arizona 85262
602 894 6231

Margo Halverson-Heywood

2005 South La Corta Drive
Tempe Arizona 85282

Margo Halverson-Heywood
Graphic Designer

Margo Halverson-Heywood
Graphic Designer

2005 South La Corta Drive
Tempe Arizona 85282
602 894 6231

Client: Avenue Edit
Design Firm: Fusion Design Associates
Designer: Fred Knapp
Art Director: Fred Knapp
Paper/Printing: Four colors on 70-lb. Hammermill Offset Opaque White Lustre

AVENUE EDIT

AVENUE EDIT

625 N MICHIGAN AVE

CHICAGO IL 60611

625 N MICHIGAN AVE

CHICAGO IL 60611

1•312•943•7100

inkworks

Richard W. Guerra
Silkscreen Printing

inkworks

2703 Gilbert Circle Arlington, Texas 76010

inkworks

Richard W. Guerra
Silkscreen Printing

2703 Gilbert Circle Arlington, Texas 76010
Metro 640-0628 Digital Pager 356-4302

2703 Gilbert Circle Arlington, Texas 76010 Metro 640-0628 Digital Pager 356-4302

Client: Far West Rice
Design Firm: Image Group
Designer: Dave Zavala
Art Director: Dave Zavala
Paper/Printing: Stationery & envelope: 24-lb. Simpson Protocol Writing, Bright White Wove;
Business Card: 88-lb. Simpson Protocol Cover Bright White Wove

KEITH M. ORME

EXECUTIVE
VICE PRESIDENT

P.O. BOX 370
DURHAM, CA. 95938
3455 NELSON ROAD
NELSON, CA. 95958
916 891 1339
FAX: 916 891 0723

P.O. BOX 370   DURHAM, CA. 95938   3455 NELSON ROAD   NELSON, CA.,95958   TEL: 916 891 1339   FAX: 916 891 0723

Client: Pacific Pastures Business System
Design Firm: Image Group, Inc.
Designer: Mark Marinozzi
Art Director: Mark Marinozzi
Paper/Printing: Stationery & envelope: Two colors and embossing on 24-lb. Neutech Ultra White;
Business Card: Two colors and embossing on Neutech Ultra White Cover

PACIFIC
PASTURES

International Food Specialty Company
248 Oak Tree Drive
Santa Rosa, California 95401
(707) 576 7940
Fax (707) 542 9354

Client: Watson Photography
Design Firm: Rickabaugh Graphics
Designer: Mark Krumel
Art Director: Mark Krumel
Paper/Printing: Two colors on textured stock

Client: Brad Bean Photography
Design Firm: The Weller Institute for the Cure of Design
Designer: Don Weller
Art Director: Don Weller
Paper/Printing: Two colors on Beckett Cambric White

Client: Downtown Typography
Design Firm: Stan Evenson Design
Designer: Stan Evenson
Art Director: Stan Evenson
Paper/Printing: Two colors, embossed on Classic Crest White

TYPOGRAPHY AND PRINTING

TYPOGRAPHY AND PRINTING

855 N. CAHUENGA BOULEVARD
LOS ANGELES, CALIFORNIA
90038

1220 MAPLE AVENUE
LOS ANGELES, CA 90015
213-749-7569
213-749-1151
FAX 213-749-9338

Client: Prodigy Services Corp.
Design Firm: Peterson & Blyth Associates
Designer: Ronald Peterson
Art Director: Ronald Peterson
Paper/Printing: Two colors

Prodigy Services Company
445 Hamilton Avenue
White Plains, NY 10601
Telephone (914) 993-8000

PRODIGY.
Interactive Personal Service

PRODIGY.
Interactive Personal Service

Prodigy Services Company
445 Hamilton Avenue
White Plains, NY 10601

Client: Integrated Media Systems
Design Firm: Russell Leong Design
Designer: Russell K. Leong, Pam Matsuda
Art Director: Russell K. Leong
Paper/Printing: Black plus three fluorescent colors on white

Client: Main Street Toy Company, Inc.
Design Firm: McKinlay & Partners
Creative Director: Lee A. Hill
Art Director: Jennifer Kelley
Paper/Printing: Two colors on Strathmore White Writing

Main Street Toy

The Main Street Toy Company, Inc.
P.O. Box 700 • West Simsbury, CT 06092
(203) 651-4986

Main Street Toy

Fred T. Heine
Vice President

The Main Street Toy Company, Inc.
P.O. Box 700 • West Simsbury, CT 06092
(203) 651-4986 • Fax (203) 232-4033

Main Street Toy

The Main Street Toy Company, Inc.
P.O. Box 700 • West Simsbury, CT 06092

Client: Robert Stolkin Photography
Design Firm: Akagi Design
Designers: Doug Akagi, Lydia Young
Art Director: Doug Akagi
Paper/Printing: Stationery & Envelope: Two colors on 28-lb. Strathmore Writing Fluorescent White Wove;
Business Card: Two colors on 10 pt. Kromekote 2S

Client: Mascot Developments Ltd.
Design Firm: WM de Majo Associates
Designer: WM de Majo, MBE FCSD
Art Director: WM de Majo, MBE FCSD
Paper/Printing: Four colors

MASCOT DEVELOPMENTS LTD
Registered office:
77 Borough Road, London SE1 1DW Telephone: 01-407 8891 Telex 884498

A subsidiary of *Charles Letts (Holdings) Ltd*, registered in England No. 1835581
Directors: T.R. Letts, Chairman & Managing, A.A. Letts, D.F. Denby FCIS

Client: Beckett Paper Company
Design Firm: Rickabaugh Graphics
Designer: Eric Rickabaugh
Art Director: Eric Rickabaugh
Paper/Printing: Three colors with emboss on 24-lb. Beckett Text Writing Harbor Mist

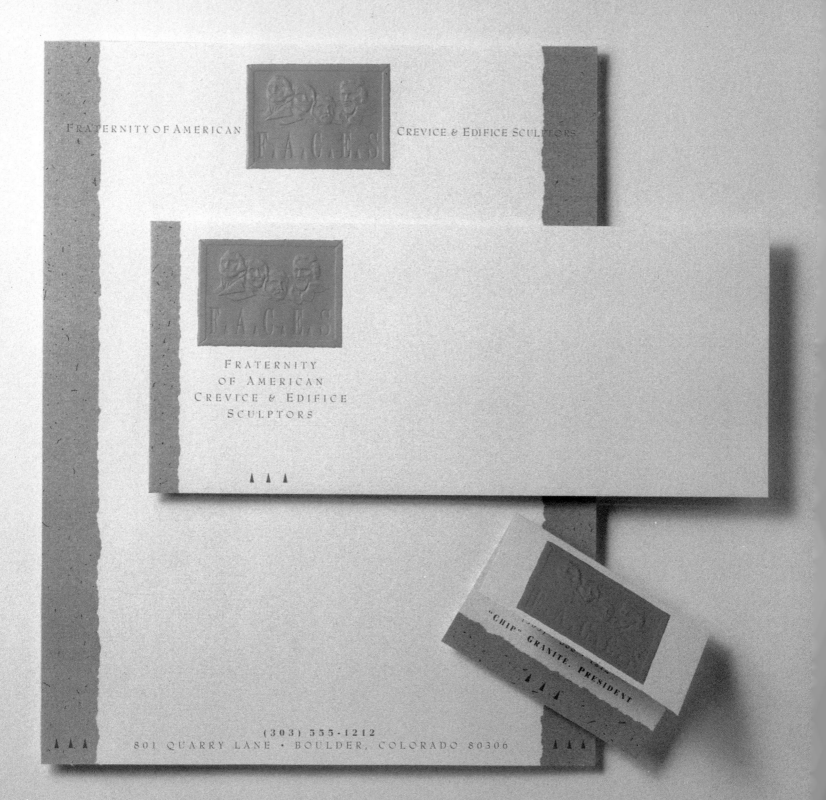

Client: Janet Gentile Sales
Design Firm: Marks/Bielenberg Design
Designer: John Bielenberg
Art Director: John Bielenberg
Paper/Printing: One color plus die-cut four-color sticker on 24-lb. Strathmore Bright White Writing

Client: Apac Corporation/Radio America
Design Firm: Bullet Communications
Designer: Tim Scott
Art Director: Tim Scott
Paper/Printing: Four colors on 24-lb. Protocol Bright White
Writing Wove

Client: Marlin Estates, Ltd.
Design Firm: Jonn Nash & Friends
Designer: Peta Nash
Art Director: John Nash
Paper/Printing: Two colors on White Conqueror

RADIO AMERICA

MARLIN ESTATES
LIMITED

New Richmond
SUPPLY LAUNDRIES

NEW · SOUTH · WALES · MODEL
YACHTING · ASSOCIATION

ALL · CORRESPONDENCE · TO

Client: New Richmond Supply Laundries
Design Firm: Tim Girvin Design, Inc.
Designer: Mary Radosevich
Art Director: Tim Girvin
Paper/Printing: Two colors plus silver foil on Strathmore
Bright White Writing Wove

Client: N.S.W. Model Yachting Association
Design Firm: Raymond Bennett Design Pty. Ltd.
Designer: Raymond Bennett
Art Director: Raymond Bennett
Paper/Printing: One color on 85 gsm bond

Title: Letterhead for Aaronite/Morceau Limited
Design Firm: John Nash & Friends
Designer: John Nash
Art Director: John Nash
Paper/Printing: Three-color process

Aaronite Limited

Viking Close
Willerby
Hull HU10 6DS

Telephone
(0482) 659381

Telex
597574

Fax
(0482) 650498

PASSIVE FIRE PROTECTORS

AARONITE

Your Ref
Our Ref
Date

A subsidiary company of Morceau Holdings plc Registered in England no. 1188143 Registered office Viking Close Willerby Hull HU10 6DS Vat no. 347511945
Directors R.G. Neilson (Managing), P.A. Wrigley, P.M. Whicher, R.J. Donaldson

Client: Applied Medical Systems
Design Firm: Corey McPherson Nash
Designer: Susan Gilzow
Art Director: Susan Gilzow
Paper/Printing: Two colors plus copper foil on Protocol Writing Gray

Client: Morren + Barkin
Design Firm: Virginia Morren Design
Designer: Virginia Morren
Art Director: Virginia Morren
Paper/Printing: Two colors

Client: Giscal Hair & Make-up
Design Firm: Visual Due Studio
Designer: Vittorio Prina
Art Director: Vittorio Prina
Paper/Printing Two colors on gloss enamel stock

Client: A&I Color Laboratory
Design Firm: Butler Kosh Brooks
Designer: Larry Brooks
Art Director: Butler Kosh Brooks
Paper/Printing: Three colors

Client: Micromet
Design Firm: Primo Angeli Inc.
Designers: Ray Honda Doug Hardenbaugh Mark Jones
Art Director: Primo Angeli
Paper/Printing: Two colors with registered emboss on 70-lb Curtis Brightwater Text

Client: Dallas Repertory Theatre
Design Firm: Peterson & Company
Designer: Scott Ray
Art Director: Scott Ray
Paper/Printing: Three colors on Strathmore Bright White

Client: Silverblade Services Ltd
Design Firm: John Nash & Friends
Designer: John Nash
Art Director: John Nash
Paper/Printing: Two colors on White Conqueror

Client: Century Toyota
Design Firm: Stan Evenson Design
Designer: Stan Evenson Design
Art Director: Stan Evenson Design
Paper/Printing: Two colors on 24-lb. Strathmore Bright White

Client: Drukkerij Mart.Spruijt bv
Design Firm: Samenwerkende Ontwerpers
Designer: Theo Nijsse
Art Director: Marianne Vos

drukkerij **MART.SPRUIJT** bv

Dynamostraat 7

1014 BN Amsterdam

Telefoon 020 - 84 94 95

Telefax 020 - 86 09 36

'Prijsopgave,
transacties
en leveringen
geschieden
volgens de
leveringsvoor-
waarden voor
de grafische
industrie,
gedeponeerd
ter griffie van de
arrondissements-
rechtbank te
amsterdam,
een exemplaar
wordt op
aanvraag
toegezonden.'

Handelsregister 9925 · Nederlandsche Middenstandsbank Herengracht 580 nr 69.74.61.904 · Postgiro 89926

Client: Souper Salad
Design Firm: Midnight Oil Studios
Designers: Midnight Oil Studios
Art Directors: Midnight Oil Studios
Paper/Printing: Two color thermography on 24-lb. Howard Linen

· 8   O ·
A S H F O R D
S T R E E T
B O S T O N
MASSACHUSETTS
O   2   1   3   4
(617) 254-SOUP
FAX 2 5 4 - 7 6 1 3

Design Firm: Butler Kosh Brooks
Designers: Butler Kosh Brooks
Art Directors: Butler Kosh Brooks
Paper/Printing: Four-color process on Curtis Brightwater, rib laid finish

Client: Mike Salisbury Communications
Design Firm: Mike Salisbury Communications
Designers: Mike Salisbury, Cindy Luck
Illustrators: Pam Hamilton, W.T. Vinson
Art Director: Mike Salisbury

P.O. REQUEST —

INVOICE

INVOICE:

DATE:

OUR JOB #:

YOUR P.O. #:

MIKE

SALISBURY

■ MIKE SALISBURY COMMUNICATION   TORRANCE CA 90501   213 320-7660

■ MIKE SALISBURY COMMUNICATIONS 2200   ANCE CA 90501

FAX

FACSIMILE COVER LETTER

Please deliver the following pages to:

NAME:_____

FIRM:_____

FROM:_____

We are transmitting a total of _____ pages, following this cover page.

DATE:_____

TIME:_____

If you do not receive all the pages, please call (213) 320-7660 and ask for:

Transmitting on a Xerox telecopier at (213) 320-4779

■ MIKE SALISBURY COMMUNICATIONS 2200 AMAPOLA CT   TORRANCE CA 90501   213 320-7660

MIKE SALISBURY COMMUNICATIONS 2200 AMAPOLA CT TORRANCE CA 90501 213 320-7660

MEMO

MIKE SALISBURY

2 2 0 0
A M A P O L A
C O U R T
TORRANCE, CA
9 0 5 0 1
213 320-7660

Le Louvre vous offre ces documents pour préparer votre visite

LOUVRE

Service culturel

MINISTÈRE DE LA CULTURE, DE LA COMMUNICATION, DES GRANDS TRAVAUX ET DU BICENTENAIRE

Administration Générale

LOUVRE

LOUVRE

Musée du Louvre
75058 Paris Cedex 01
Téléphone (1) 40 20 50 50
Télécopie (1) 42 60 45 43

LOUVRE

Musée du Louvre
34-36 Quai du Louvre
75058 Paris Cedex 01
Téléphone (1) 40 20 50 50
Télécopie (1) 42 60 45 43

LOUVRE

Service de la Communication

Patricia Mounier

Musée du Louvre
34-36 Quai du Louvre
75058 Paris Cedex 01
Téléphone (1) 40 20 51 51

Design Firm: David Westwood & Associates
Designer: David Westwood
Art Director: David Westwood
Paper/Printing: One color on White Classic Crest

Design Firm: Storms Design Group
Designers: Storms Design Group
Art Director: Storms Design Group
Paper/Printing: One color plus foil on Strathmore Writing

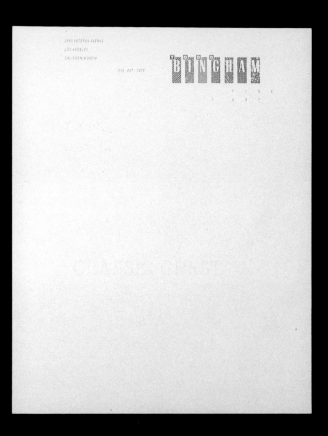

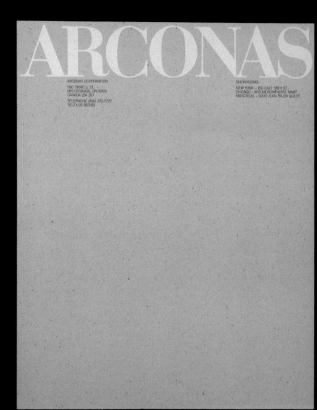

Client: Lori Adamski-Peek
Design Firm: The Weller Institute for the Cure of Design, Inc.
Designer: Don Weller
Art Director: Don Weller
Paper/Printing: Two colors on White Classic Crest

Client: Arconas Corporation
Design Firm: Raymond Lee & Associates Limited
Designer: Raymond Lee
Art Director: Raymond Lee
Paper/Printing: Two colors

DESTINATIONS

Client: Europa Products, Inc.
Design Firm: The Thompson Design Group
Designers: Dennis Thompson, Elizabeth Berta
Art Directors: Dennis Thompson, Jody Thompson
Paper/Printing: 1/color on Strathmore Writing

Client: The Fitness Factory
Design Firm: Debra Malinics Advertising
Designers: Debra Malinics, Mary Kay Garttmeier
Art Directors: Debra Malinics, Mary Kay Garttmeier
Paper/Printing: Two colors on Strathmore Bond

Client: Midnight Oil Studios
Design Firm: Midnight Oil Studios
Paper/Printing: Four colors on 60-lb. Mohawk Vellum Cream/White

51 MELCHER ST.
B O S T O N
MASSACHUSETTS
0 2 2 1 0
U S A
P H O N E
(617) 350-7970
F A X
(617) 350-7971

51 MELCHER ST.
BOSTON,
MASSACHUSETTS
02210
(617) 350-7970

JAMES
SKILES

51
MELCHER ST.
BOSTON, MA 02210
(617) 350-7970

Client: Travel Clinic of San Antonio
Design Firm: Taylor/Christian Advertising
Designer: Roger Christian
Illustrator: David Hackney
Paper/Printing: Stationery: Four colors on 24-lb. Protocol Writing White Wove;
Envelope: One color on 70-lb. Speckletone Natural Text with a
foreign stamped affixed; Business Card: Three colors on 88-lb. Protocol White

Client: Hillis & Mackey Company
Design Firm: Hillis & Mackey Company
Designer: Terry Mackey
Art Director: Terry Mackey
Paper/Printing: Three colors on white bond

Hillis
Mackey
COMPANY

1550 UTICA AVENUE SOUTH • SUITE 745 • MINNEAPOLIS, MN 55416 • 612-542-9122

Hillis
Mackey
COMPANY

1550 UTICA AVE. S. • SUITE 745
MINNEAPOLIS, MN 55416

Hillis
Mackey
COMPANY

1550 UTICA AVE. S. • SUITE 745
MINNEAPOLIS, MN 55416

612-542-9122

Client: Barbara Gilman Gallery
Design Firm: Michael Wolk Design
Designer: Michael Wolk
Art Director: Michael Wolk
Paper/Printing: Two colors on Strathmore Bright White Writing

270 Northeast 39th Street

Miami, Florida 33137

Telephone 305.573.4898

Facsimile 305.576.1839

270 Northeast 39th Street

Miami, Florida 33137

Telephone 305.573.4898

Facsimile 305.576.1839

BARBARA GILLMAN GALLERY

BARBARA GILLMAN GALLERY

Client: Flora Verdé Flowers
Design Firm: Boelts Brothers Design, Inc.
Designers: Jackson Boelts, Eric Boelts
Art Directors: Jackson Boelts, Eric Boelts
Paper/Printing: Three colors on Cranes Crest 24-lb. White Wove

Client: Michael Linley Illustration
Design Firm: Rickabaugh Graphics
Designer: Eric Rickabaugh
Art Director: Eric Rickabaugh
Paper/Printing: Two colors

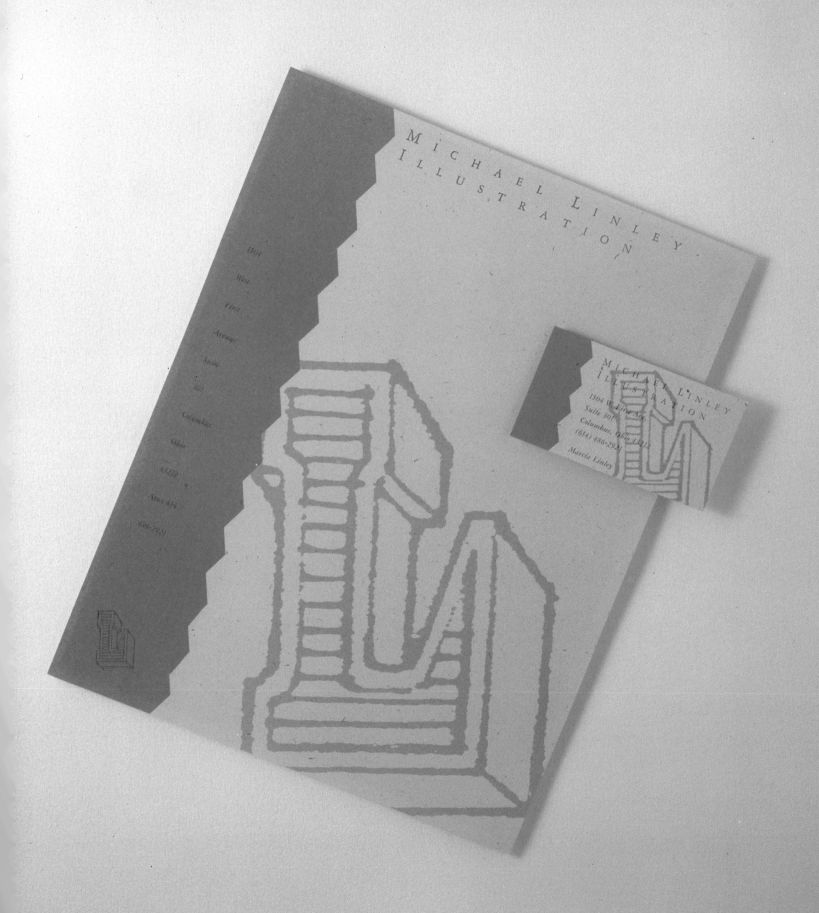

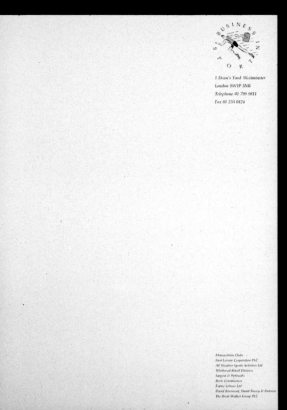

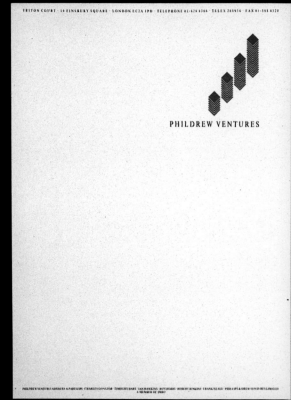

Client: Westminster Strategy
Design Firm: Leslie Millard Associates
Designer: Ian McLaren
Art Director: Les Causton
Paper/Printing: Printed in two colors on white bond

Client: Phildrew Ventures
Design Firm: John Nash & Friends
Designer: John Nash
Art Director: John Nash
Paper/Printing: Two colors

Client: Jim Laser Photography
Design Firm: Hornall Anderson Design Works
Designers: Jack Anderson, Raymond Terada
Art Director: Jack Anderson

L A S E R

J I M   L A S E R
P H O T O G R A P H E R

T H E   L A S E R   W O R K S
A T E L I E R   P H O T O G R A P H I Q U E

WILDWOOD BEACH·HANSVILLE·WASHINGTON 98340
2 0 6   6 3 8 - 2 1 3 1

Client: Peter Darley Miller Photography
Design Firm: Bright & Associates
Designer: James Marrin
Art Director: James Marrin
Paper/Printing: Two colors and die-cut on Protocol 100

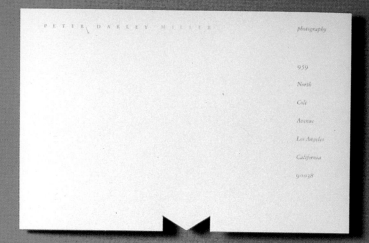

Client: Forest Hill Vineyard
Design Firm: Primo Angeli Inc.
Designer: Ray Honda
Art Director: Primo Angeli

F O R E S T   H I L L   V I N E Y A R D

. KATHRYN COLE MANACE
VICE-PRESIDENT/
SALES AND MARKETING

FOREST HILL VINEYARD
P.O. BOX 96 ST. HELENA
CALIFORNIA 94574
415-386-2559

P.O. BOX 96
ST. HELENA
CALIFORNIA
94574 .

F O R E S T   H I L L   V I N E Y A R D

P.O. BOX 96
ST. HELENA
CALIFORNIA
94574
707-963-7229
ST. HELENA
415-386-2559
SAN FRANCISCO

GRASS
TRIPLES
TOURNAMENTS

Client: FGE/KVGO
Design Firm: Samenwerkende Ontwerpers
Designer: André Toet
Art Director: André Toet

Client: El Cinematographo
Design Firm: Medina Design
Designer: Fernando Medina
Art Director: Fernando Medina

Client: Winsted Volleyball Club
Design Firm: Gormley & Welker Graphic Design
Designer: Tim Gormley
Art Director: Steve Welker

EL CINEMATOGRAFO

Client: Midwest Old Threshers
Design Firm: Macuk + Associates
Designer: Barbara Aden
Art Director: Kent Mauck

Client: Danbury Music Centre
Design Firm: Gormley & Welker Graphic Design
Designer: Tim Gormley
Art Director: Steve Welker

Client: K2 Skis
Design Firm: Hornall Anderson Design Works
Designers: Jack Anderson, Jani Drewfs, Mary Hermes
Art Director: Jack Anderson

Client: Hubbell Realty Company
Design Firm: Mauck + Associates
Designer: Barbara Aden
Art Director: Kent Mauck

Client: Advertisers Broadcast Services, Inc.
Design Firm: Bullet Communications
Designer: Tim Scott
Art Director: Tim Scott

Client: Pure Harvest Corporation
Design Firm: Image Group, Inc.
Designer: Mark Marinozzi
Art Director: Mark Marinozzi

Client: Tennis Training Center
Design Firm: UCI, Inc.
Designer: Don Sato
Art Director: Roy Urano

Client: Consolidated-Bathurst Inc.
Design Firm: Rolf Harder & Associates
Designer: Rolf Harder
Art Director: Rolf Harder

ALFA 164

CELEBRITY RACE

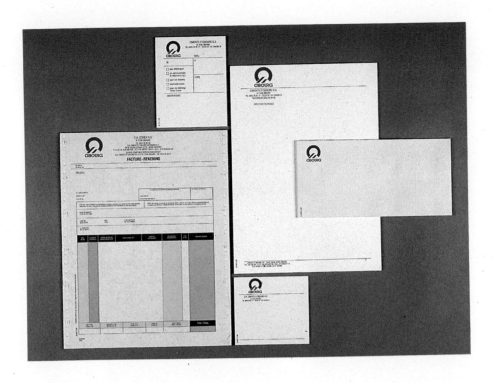

Client: Alfa Romeo
Design Firm: Carter Wong Limited
Designer: Fiona Barlow
Art Directors: Philip Wong, Nick Downes

Client: Ciments D'Obourg
Design Firm: Design Board
Behaegel & Partners
Designers: Denis Keller, Erik Vantal
Art Director: Denis Keller

Client: RTBF/Eurovision
Design Firm: Design Board
Behaegel & Partners
Designers: Eric Huber
Art Director: Dennis Keller

Client: Charles Salter Associates, Inc.
Design Firm: Cahan & Associates
Designer: Kathy Warriner
Art Director: Bill Cahan
Paper/Printing: Four colors (folder) and five colors (all others). Proposal Cover: 88-lb. Strathmore Writing Cover Bristol Bright White Wove; Envelope: 24-lb. Converted Strathmore Writing Bright White Wove; Business Card: 88-lb. Strathmore Writing Cover Bristol Bright White Wove; Label: 80-lb. Starliner Scenario White uncoated litho vellum

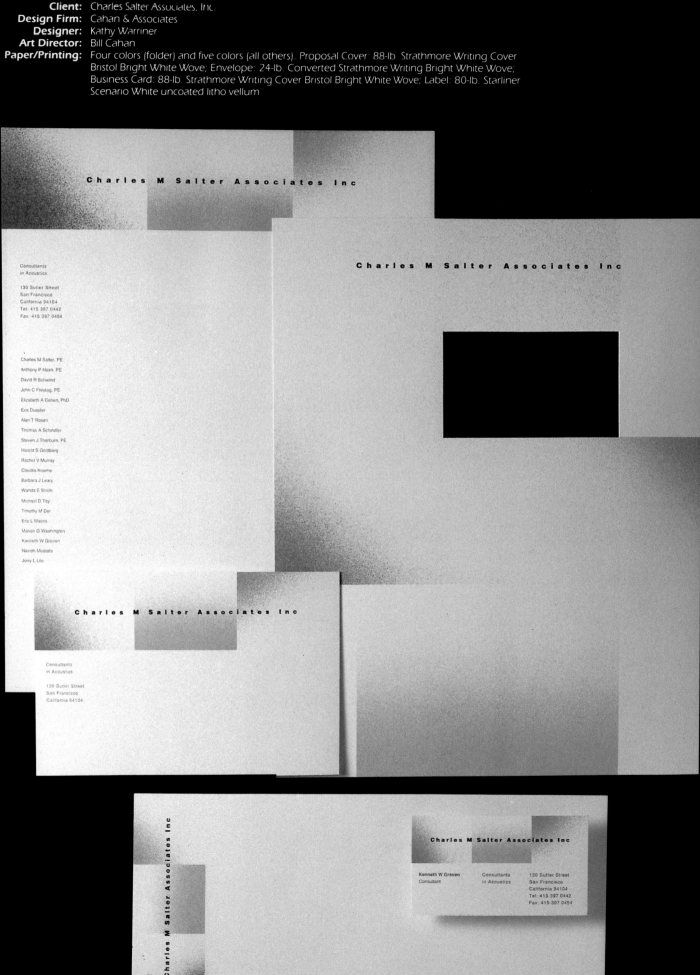

Client: Tucson Arts District
Design Firm: Boelts Bros. Design/Mike Gross Design Concepts
Designers: Jackson Boelts, Eric Boelts, Mike Gross
Paper/Printing: Two colors on 24-lb. Gainsborough Frost Text

Client: Scripts & Concepts, Inc.
Design Firm: Rickabaugh Graphics
Designer: Eric Rickabaugh
Art Director: Eric Rickabaugh
Paper/Printing: One color plus copper foil

Client: McKinlay & Partners
Design Firm: McKinlay & Partners
Designer: David Martino
Art Director: David Martino
Paper/Printing: Three colors

Design Firm: Jukka Veistola
Designers: Jukka Veistola, Matti Sivonen
Art Director: Jukka Veistola
Paper/Printing: One color on White Conqueror

Design Firm: Corey McPherson Nash
Designers: Terry Dobson, Marian Heibel, Tim Nihope
Art Director: Scott Nash
Paper/Printing: Three colors on Strathmore Writing Wove

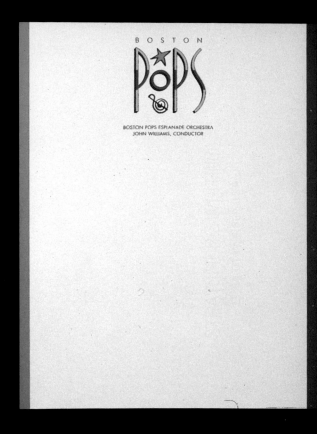

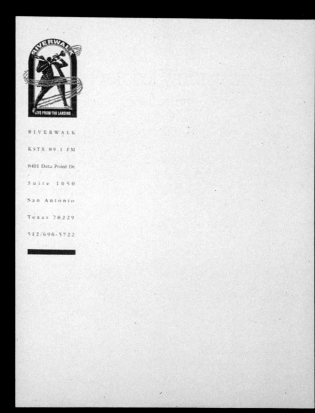

Client: Harry Metzler Artdesign
Design Firm: Harry Metzler Artdesign
Designer: Harry Metzler
Art Director: Harry Metzler
Paper/Printing: Two colors

Client: Riverwalk/KSTX Radio
Design Firm: The Bradford Lawton Design Group, Inc.
Designers: Bradford Lawton, Jody Laney, Ellen Pullen
Art Directors: Bradford Lawton, Jody Laney, Ellen Pullen
Paper/Printing: Litho black and thermograph blue on
Protocol Bright White Wove

Client: Marco Pirovano, photographer
Design Firm: Visual Due Studio
Designer: Vittorio Prina
Art Director: Vittorio Prina

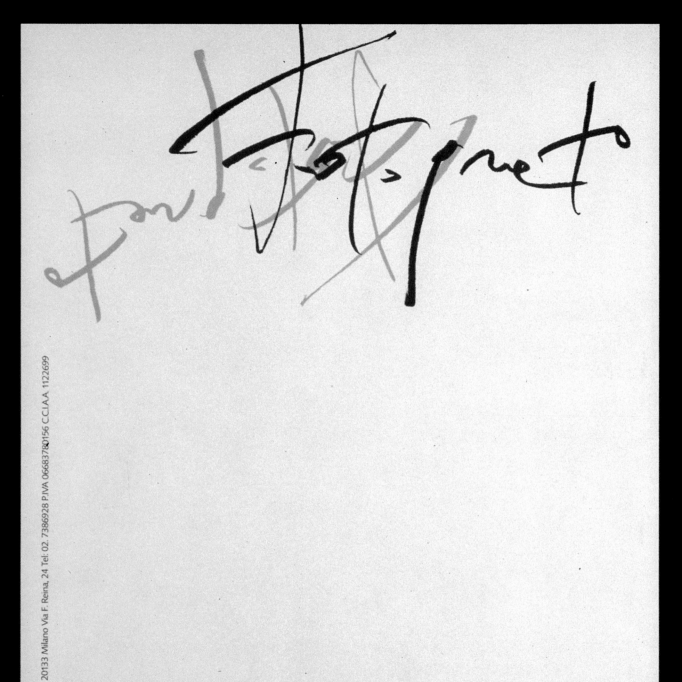

20133 Milano Via F. Reina, 24 Tel: 02. 7386928 P.IVA 06683780156 C.C.I.A.A. 1122699

Marco Pirovano

Client: The Symington Company
Design Firm: Hubbard and Hubbard Design
Designer: Julie Henson
Art Director: Ann Morton Hubbard
Paper/Printing: Two colors on Speckletone Madera Beach

Client: Lockard Inc.
Design Firm: Graphic Editions
Designers: Logo: Joy Bievenour; Layout: Todd Burgard
Art Director: Nancy Miller
Paper/Printing: Three colors on 80-lb. Curtis Bright Water Bright White Text

Client: Habiter 87
Design Firm: Graphus
Designer: Fokke Draaijer
Art Director: Pierre Bernard

Client: Paco
Design Firm: Alan Chan Design Co.
Designers: Alan Chan, Phillip Leung
Art Director: Alan Chan

PACO KAWANA
FLAT 4A 6/F
146 TAI HANG ROAD
HONG KONG
RES 5-8904399
OFFICE 5-260904
FAX 5-8453449

WITH COMPLIMENTS

PACO KAWANA
FLAT 4A 6/F
146 TAI HANG ROAD
HONG KONG
RES 5-8904399
OFFICE 5-260904
FAX 5-8453449

PACO KAWANA
FLAT 4A 6/F
146 TAI HANG ROAD
HONG KONG
RES 5-8904399
OFFICE 5-260904
FAX 5-8453449

PAVILION MALL

Management
Office

17900
Southcenter
Parkway
Suite 227
Tukwila, WA
98188

(206) 575-8090

Leasing/
Marketing

Trammell Crow
Company
P.O. Box 80326
Seattle, WA
98108

(206)762-4750

WINE

MENU

Beppis

RISTORANTE

Beppis

ANTIPASTI FREDDI

OYSTERS NATURAL
half shell with cocktail sauce
½ doz. 6.50   doz. 9.90

OYSTERS FRIED
with lemon, parsley & tartare sauce
½ doz. 7.20   doz. 11.90

ANTIPASTO PRIMAVERA
marinated & pickled vegetables
8.20

OCTOPUS MARINATI AL LIMONE
marinated in oil, parsley & bayleaf
8.20

CARPACCIO DI TONNO
sliced raw tuna & horseradish
10.90

ZUPPE

STRACCIATELLA ROMANA
chicken stock with egg & cheese
6.50

MINESTRONE
Italian mixed vegetables
6.50

PASTA CASALINGHA

TAGLIATELLE CON VONGOLE
baby clams & tomato
11.90   14.90

LASAGNE AL FORNO
baked pasta, meat & ricotta cheese
8.50   12.50

SPAGHETTI ALLA MARINARA
mixed seafood & tomato sauce
11.90   14.90

SPAGHETTI ALLA CARBONARA
bacon, cheese & egg sauce
8.50   12.50

TORTELLINI AL FUNGHETTO
mushrooms & cream
8.50   12.50

PAGLIA E FIENO
prosciutto, cream & nutmeg
8.50   12.50

POLLAMI

FILLET OF CHICKEN ROSMARINO
brandy, rosemary, cream & mustard
16.90

BREAST OF CHICKEN PIZZAIOLA
tomato, capers & wine
16.90

RISTORANTE

Beppis

WITH COMPLIMENTS

Corner Yurong and Stanley Street
East Sydney NSW Australia 2010

Corner Yurong and Stanley Street East Sydney NSW Australia 2010 Telephone: (02) 360 4558

RISTORANTE

Beppis

G. BEPPI POLESE
Corner Yurong and Stanley Street
East Sydney NSW Australia 2010
Telephone: (02) 360 4558

Client: Yankeetown Thoroughbreds
Design Firm: Rickabaugh Graphics
Designer: Mark Krumel
Art Director: Mark Krumel
Paper/Printing: Two colors

4246 SUNBURY ROAD
GALENA, OHIO 43021

DOUGLAS A. SNYDER,
OWNER

FARM
4246 SUNBURY ROAD
GALENA, OHIO 43021
614-965-2553

BUSINESS OFFICE
692 N. HIGH STREET
SUITE 201
COLUMBUS, OHIO 43215
614-464-2601

Client: Gilbert Investments
Design Firm: Tim Girvin Design, Inc.
Designer: Chris Spivey
Art Director: Tim Girvin
Paper/Printing: One color plus gold foil on Strathmore Writing

Gilbert
Investments
Limited

3805
Hunts
Point
Road

Bellevue
Washington
98004

Gilbert Investments Limited	3805 Hunts Point Road	Bellevue Washington 98004 206.451.8722	Gilbert G. Eade

Client: Université de Franche-Comté
Design Firm: Catherine Zask
Designer: Catherine Zask
Art Director: Catherine Zask
Paper/Printing: Five colors

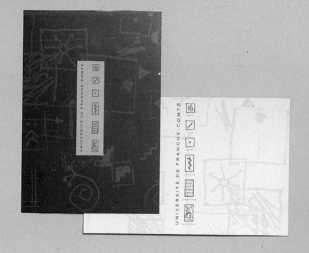

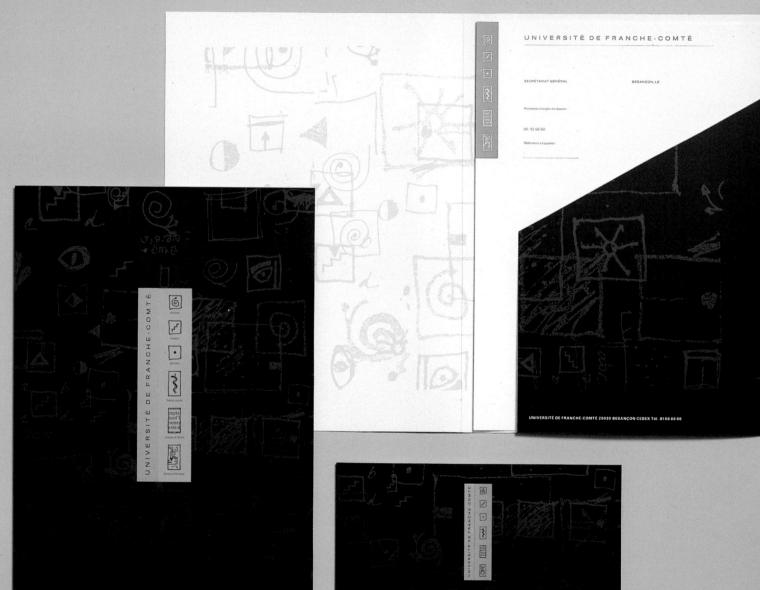

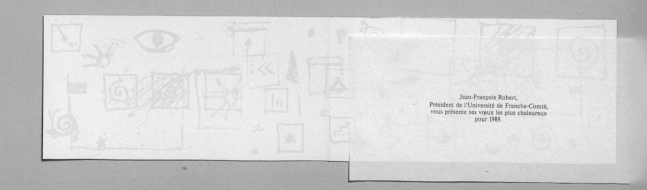

Client: Holiday Junction Corporation
Design Firm: Raymond Lee & Associates Limited
Designer: Raymond Lee
Illustrators: Derek Chung, Tiam Fook
Paper/Printing: Four colors on white stock, laid finish

Client: Skan/Michael Smith
Design Firm: Margo Halverson-Heywood
Designer: Margo Halverson-Heywood
Paper/Printing: Three colors on 28-lb. Classic Crest Writing

Skan International
Network for
Reichian Work

Michael Smith
Co-founder

RR2 Box 271
Santa Fe
New Mexico 87505
505 473 0559

Hohe Bleichen 26
2 Hamburg 36
West Germany
49 40 345163

Michael Smith
Skan International
Network for
Reichian Work

RR2 Box 271
Santa Fe
New Mexico 87505

Hohe Bleichen 26
2 Hamburg 36
West Germany

Skan International
Network for
Reichian Work

Michael Smith
Co-founder

Client: Designosaurus Rex
Design Firm: Designosaurus Rex
Designer: Rex Morache
Art Director: Rex Morache
Paper/Printing: Two-colors. Stationery: 20-lb. bond stock, Business card: 10 pt. Kromekote Cover, Mailer: 80-lb. cover—Tahoe